Dixie Before Disney

HATCHERIES AT LYMAN
BIG BILOXI RIVER RECREATIONAL AREA
49
MILK OF MAGNESIA PLANT
DAIRIES
FISHING CAMPS
LITE NIGHTS
COTTON COMPRESS AND WAREHOUSE
I.C.R.R.
WGCM
AIRPORT
A.N.G. JET TRAINING
2 GOLF COURSES
"BEAUVO
SULLIVAN-RYAN FIGHT 1882
VETERAN HOSPITAL
TRAILER COUNTRY
SEA-BEES
GULF PARK
OLLEGE FOR GIRLS
WATER BALLET)
CITY PARK
LLBURNED 1956
MARINE LIFE
Edgewate
Park
YACHT CLUB
OLD SPANISH TRAIL
Mississippi City
90
Long Beach
Gulfport
GIGGING FO
FLOUNDE
BY LANTE
FISHING JETTY
THROW NET FISHING FOR MULLET
SAILING REGATTAS
ACHTING
849
FLYING FISHING
Gulf
EXCURSION BOAT GULFPORT TO SHIP ISLAND
DEEP

Dixie Before Disney

100 Years of Roadside Fun

Tim Hollis

University Press of Mississippi
Jackson

Dedicated to the memory of my father,
Lynn S. Hollis (1930-1995),
from whom I inherited my love
for the tourist attractions and
roadside landscape of the South.

http://www.upress.state.ms.us

Copyright © 1999 by Tim Hollis
All rights reserved
Manufactured in the United States of America

Designed by Todd Lape

02 01 00 99   4 3 2 1

Library of Congress Cataloging-in-
Publication Data
Hollis, Tim.

Dixie before Disney: 100 Years of Roadside Fun /
Tim Hollis.
p.   cm.
Includes bibliographical references and index.
ISBN 1-57806-117-2 (cloth : alk. paper). – ISBN
1-57806-118-0 (paper : alk. paper)
1. Tourist trade–Southern States–History.
2. Southern States–Description and
travel–History.
I. Title
G155.U6H58   1999
338.4'791750443–dc21   98-35708
CIP

British Library Cataloging-in-Publication Data
available

Printed in Canada

Contents

Acknowledgments

This book could not have been completed without the cooperation of the individuals who make up the tourism industry of today, and those who founded the industry in years past. Most attractions and businesses I contacted were more than eager to share their knowledge with me; however, there were some who acted like I had just dropped in from another planet. In the text, if certain areas seem to be lacking in detail, it is usually because no one was able to help dig up anything else to say.

At any rate, the number of those who were helpful far exceeds the number of those who were not. In no particular order, I would like to thank: Jim Antone (Horne's history); Steve Specht (Silver Springs & Weeki Wachee Springs); the Ocala, Florida, Chamber of Commerce; Bill Stuckey Jr.; Marla Akin; Brian Rheawinkel (Florida Department of Tourism); Richard Wineburger (Ripley's Believe It Or Not Museum, Gatlinburg); Cindy Keller (Land of Oz); Steve Petermann (Gulfarium); Robyn DeRidder (Cypress Gardens); Bill Chapin and Todd Smith (Rock City Gardens); the Uncle Remus Museum, Eatonton, Ga.; Mary Jaeger-Gale (Chimney Rock); Dottie Locke (Potter's Wax Museum); Mrs. Rede Douglas of Gatlinburg; JoAnn Leight (Dinosaur Land); Michael Goldstein (Busch Gardens); Fred Thumberg (Fairyland of Tampa); Janet Alford (McKee Jungle Gardens); Marineland of Florida; Frank Craddock of Pensacola, Fla.; Cora Saxon; Donnie Pitchford (Mountain Village 1890); the National Lum & Abner Society (Dick Huddleston's Store); Steve Gilmer; Donna Ross (Florida Attractions Association); Len Davidson and Jim Hiett (roadside giant statues); Dwight Wilson (Jacksonville Beach Historical Society); Cliff Holman; Jim Sidwell Sr. (Magic World); Barbara Crews (*Southern Living* Magazine); Bill Hardman (Southeastern Tourism Association); Dr. Brian Rucker; Chris Robbins (Land of Oz/Tweetsie Railroad/Goldrush Junction); Alta Love and Bob Fleske (Goofy Golf); the Anna Porter Public Library, Gatlinburg; Randy Sheffield; Marbie Geller of the Cape Coral, Fla., Historical Museum; Carole Griffin (Miami Seaquarium); Grandfather Mountain; the Cherokee, N.C., Visitors' Center; Wallace Hebert of JRN, Inc.; Beverly Hunter (Sarasota Jungle Gardens); Ellen Long (Dollywood); Joanna Norman, Florida State Archives; Nancy Jane Tetzlaff (Jungle Larry's Safari); Gene Aiken, Gatlinburg, Tenn.; Ed Tennyson; Kay

Powell (Pigeon Forge Department of Tourism); Jim Clark; Jim Johnstone (Icee Corporation); Ann Elstad (*Georgia* magazine); R. B. Coburn (Ghost Town/Six Gun Territory/Frontier Land); Whistle Stop Antiques, Irondale, Ala.; Randy Koplin (Goofy Golf and Tombstone Territory); Shirley Coleman (Roanoke, Va., Chamber of Commerce); Vincent "Val" Valentine (Jungle Land); Gordon Ewald; and Paul Churchwell (Petticoat Junction).

I would also like to extend my gratitude to my fellow roadside history authors Michael Wallis, John Baeder, Michael Karl Witzel, Lucinda Lewis, and John Margolies, for their help and encouragement during this book's long germination process.

Introduction

Ah'm from the South!! The only cups I drink out of are Dixie cups!!

—Senator Beauregard Claghorn

The book you are about to read is one I started working on when I was three years old.

Now, before you decide that either (1) this is going to be an awfully juvenile effort, or (2) it sure takes me a *long* time to get a project done, I will explain what I mean. The Southern roadside environment was always a major part of my life. Since I entered the world in 1963, right at the tail end of the baby boom era, I did not get to see firsthand the gradual development of tourism in the South. But this was compensated by the fact that I *did* get to see the South's attractions and tourist traps at the very peak of their pre-theme park frenzy.

My first experiences with the South's highways came soon after I was born in Birmingham, Alabama. My parents had friends who lived near Nashville, Tennessee, so we found ourselves traveling there occasionally. It should come as no surprise to learn that my memories of those overnight excursions are quite vague.

However, one indelible image haunted the recesses of my mind for decades.

Through the thickening haze of the passage of time, I could make out the form of a sign . . . a neon sign . . . an *enormous* neon sign depicting the famous Howard Johnson's "Simple Simon & the Pieman" logo, lighting up the night sky in a blaze of color. My recollection was that this sign was mounted on the roof of a building, not like the smaller neon versions of the logo that adorned the restaurants' signs. I carried that phantom in my fevered brain for more than 30 years, with only the foggiest idea that it had existed somewhere in Tennessee. Finally, after three decades of wondering, I happened to talk to roadside enthusiast Jim Hiett of Nashville, and told him what I thought I remembered. Thank goodness, he confirmed that such a neon spectacular had indeed existed at one time, on old U.S. 41 between Nashville and Murfreesboro! (All too typically, it is no longer there today.) I was considerably relieved to learn that this picture that had been imprinted in my mind during my first couple of years of life was not simply the product of an overactive imagination.

The author wearing a Great Smoky Mountains T-shirt from his first vacation trip.

The real turning point for me came in August 1966, when my parents finally decided to take our first official "family vacation." Inasmuch as I had no brothers or sisters, we were accompanied by my grandmother and an aunt, who held down the back seat. This being long before the days of child restraints, my position was *standing up* in the front seat, between my mom and dad. If we had been in a serious accident, I probably would not be here to write these words today; however, this did give me a great vantage point for viewing the signs and billboards that made up the roadside landscape of that era.

Our non-air-conditioned 1964 Chevrolet Biscayne pulled out of the driveway in the wee hours of the morning, in time for us to make our first breakfast stop in Chattanooga. (We did *not* "see Rock City" on that trip, but I must have observed many of their black & white painted barns along old U.S. 11 en route.) Our destination was the Great Smoky Mountains,

and it is odd how some things about that trip are still clear in my memory, while others are not. About Gatlinburg and Pigeon Forge, Tennessee, I remember nothing; I have a better recollection of Cherokee, North Carolina. We visited their dislocated western park Frontier Land (spelled as two words to keep Disney from suing them, one supposes) and the newly opened Santa's Land. At this summertime yuletide mecca, my dad insisted on taking my picture as I sat in the replica of Santa's sleigh with all nine concrete reindeer in harness. I wasn't too crazy about this idea, because I was afraid the silly thing would take off into the sky with only myself aboard to drive it! (By the way, it didn't.)

We had so much fun in the mountains that before a month had passed, we decided to take in the Gulf Coast as well. Off we were to Mobile, Alabama, and Pensacola and Fort Walton Beach, Florida. We covered a lot of ground on that trip, but I particularly remember the motel where we stayed. The Islander, as it was called, stood on a remote part of Okaloosa Island, surrounded only by sand and surf that stretched into the distance for what seemed like infinity. The Islander is still

At Santa's Land, Cherokee, North Carolina

Fort Walton Beach, Florida, in 1966. This stretch of sand is now one continuous string of motels and condominiums.

there today, but it is a high-rise condominium so hemmed in by other commercial development that it is almost invisible. Time staggers on.

So, you ask, just why did these early trips have such an influence on this book? Well, here's the key factor. For some unexplainable reason, my dad had an almost obsessive passion for saving things. Beginning with that August 1966 journey, he accumulated boxes of brochures, postcards, ticket stubs, matchbook covers, receipts, souvenirs, road maps . . . no matter where we went, he ended up saving everything. This was compounded by the fact that he was an avid amateur photographer, and must have snapped a 35mm photo of our activities every ten minutes or less.

According to a journal he kept, by the time I was seven years old we had visited at least part of virtually every major tourist area the South had to offer. (I would not see some of them, such as the Kentucky cave country and the hills of Arkansas, until some time later.)

When you consider the amount of stuff my dad saved from all of these trips combined, I had enough to write a book even before I started. In addition, I was intimately familiar with the contents of this material, as growing up it was always a lot of fun—especially on cold winter evenings—to look through all of it and reminisce about those past excursions.

As I reached my teens, I continued to tour the South, and soon fell into my dad's old habit of saving memorabilia and photographing the roadside, even after I was supposedly too old for such things as concrete dinosaurs. I don't know just when I realized that the material we had amassed was a valuable documentation of a lost era in tourism history, but, at about the same time, I discovered the wonderful world of memorabilia from even earlier days: the 1920s through the 1950s. I began making a conscious effort to increase my knowledge about the tourism industry as it was *before* the days of my personal experience with it. We almost became a part of that industry ourselves, as my dad often said that when he retired from his job as a teacher, one thing he would like to do was move somewhere and open his own motel. (The "Hollisday Inn"?) He didn't live long enough to do that, but I don't know if he was ever really serious about the idea, either.

Now, as a former United States president

was fond of saying, "I want to make one thing perfectly clear." This is not intended to be a scholarly or academic approach to Southern roadside history. Such an approach would be extremely difficult to undertake at this point in time. While there have been many fine works that examine American roadside culture from both a popular and a scholastic standpoint (see the bibliographical essays at the end of this book), few of them have paid much attention to what was going on in Dixieland. Even those that have dealt with the matter usually chose to cut their research off at the beginning of the twentieth century, totally ignoring the developments made in tourism during the 1930s and 1940s, much less (heavens to Colonel Sanders!) the 1950s and 1960s. Perhaps this volume will be the cornerstone for a whole new school of academic discussion.

Think about some of the subjects that are only hinted at here. What about the attractions that attempted to tie in with the South's pre-Civil War history? Do they give a truly accurate portrayal of that era, or are they based more upon Hollywood's image of the antebellum period? Look at the various dinosaur parks that sprang up in the post-World War II years to draw in the kiddies of the baby boom. Would a paleontologist feel comfortable at such locales as Dinosaur Land in Virginia or the now extinct Magic World in Pigeon Forge? What

about the geographically out-of-sync Wild West parks? Probably more than any other genre, they were based on a mythical image of the West that never existed . . . but why did they find such a willing clientele in the South, a thousand miles away from even the nearest region they purported to imitate? All of these topics are ripe for discussion; but there has to be a starting point somewhere, and hopefully this is it. (The very thought of an intellectual analysis of a spot such as Weeki Wachee Springs is enough to make one's head swim.)

Incidentally, anyone interested in pursuing the study of roadside history, in the South or elsewhere, should definitely be in touch with the national organization known as the Society for Commercial Archeology. This group was

The hands of time do their stuff.

Left: The Islander Motel as it appeared in 1966.

Right: The same motel, photographed in 1989. The motel has since become a condominium.

founded in 1977 to study and document the often-overlooked, and rapidly fading, elements that make up the American commercial landscape. SCA's focus is broad, taking in not only tourist attractions themselves, but also motels, restaurants, service stations, movie theatres, department stores, shopping centers, and anything else that can be found wherever automobiles congregate. Their Statement of Purpose says it well: "The purpose of the Society is to recognize the unique historical significance of the 20th century commercial built environment and cultural landscapes of North America. The Society emphasizes the impact of the automobile and the commercial process. To this end, the Society will carry out projects of documentation, education, advocacy, and conservation to encourage public awareness and understanding of these significant elements of our heritage." And they ain't just whistlin' Dixie, brother!

Let me say just a word here about the title of this book, *Dixie Before Disney*. Do not get the wrong impression: I have nothing personal against the Walt Disney Company. In fact, I have the utmost respect for the obvious creativity and talent that goes into everything they do, their theme parks included. But I think it is important to remember that, for seventy years or so, tourism in the South was tied to the region's own unique features, whereas Walt Disney World could have been built in Michigan, Maine, Iowa, or anywhere, without any significant change to its appearance.

Not every attraction that ever operated in the South will be found here. To chronicle all of them would require a volume as thick as three copies of *Gone with the Wind*. Instead, I have concentrated on those that best exemplify the major genres of Southern attractions. This book is meant as a celebration of the pre-Disney days when traveling in the South meant "See Rock City," "Stuckey's, 10 Miles," and "Silver Springs' Famous Glass Bottom Boats." Let's start now... fasten your seat belts, and for goodness sakes, *don't* let that kid stand up in the front seat!!

Dixie Before Disney

2   I Wish I Was in Dixie

I Wish I Was in Dixie

Then hoe it down and scratch your gravel,
To Dixie Land I'm bound to travel.

—Rarely-heard last verse of "Dixie"

During the past century, a number of individuals—who are otherwise well educated and literate—have observed that the North only *thought* it won the Civil War. They further explain that it was the Confederate states who actually got the best of the deal during the decades after the conflict ended, by convincing the Yankees to come to the South for their vacations and then taking all their money. Southern humorist Lewis Grizzard added his own two bits to this line of thinking: "After all," he said, "how many Southerners have you ever seen paying money to visit a reptile farm?"

Grizzard and his predecessors may not have been far from the truth. While Southerners had been aware of the unique features of their part of the country for decades, it was not until Northerners discovered those sites and began coming to visit them that the region's true tourist potential was realized. Until that time, the South was the most isolated area of the United States, known more for its place in legend than from any direct contact outsiders might have had with it.

It could be said that the first Northern visitors to come to the South in great numbers were the Union troops stationed there during the Civil War. Much fighting took place on Southern soil, of course, and between battles the soldiers had the opportunity to visit such later-famous locales as Lookout Mountain, from which it was already being reported that one could see seven states, and the beaches of the Atlantic and Gulf coasts. (As we shall see, the Civil War and its mystique would, in turn, inspire a goodly number of future roadside attractions in the South.) After the war, when some rather shady and unscrupulous individuals began slinking down from the North to profit from the defeated condition of Dixie, Southern natives got their first real contact with individuals of other backgrounds and cultures—and their impression of Northerners was probably not improved a whole lot by the integrity of the examples they were encountering.

In this book we are primarily concerned with the development of *highway* tourism in the Southern states, but it was actually the railroad, not the automobile, that first established the South as a popular vacation destination. The 1880s saw many of the era's Northern millionaires discovering that the South was a comparatively warm and balmy alternative to shivering away the winter months in their frozen native habitat. They flocked to the beaches at Jekyll Island, Georgia, and the northernmost cities of Florida's Atlantic coast. Below St. Augustine, Florida was not much more than an undeveloped wilderness, with no roads or railways carved through the jungle. Thanks to the currency crowd, that would soon change... but we will have to wait until chapter 3 to get that story.

When the automobile came down the road in the early years of the twentieth century, all of a sudden highway travel became something of a fad. Adventurous motorists took pride in setting out on marathon journeys into heretofore unseen parts of the country. Those who decided to motor toward the Southern states soon found out one of the main reasons that part of the country was so heretofore unseen: the roads in the South were among the most poorly maintained in the nation. Up to that point, they had been used primarily for farm wagons, not touring cars. In 1908, it took mapmaker R. H. Johnston 25 days to travel from Philadelphia to Savannah, Georgia, while prepar-

ing the first AAA tour guidebook to the South. Road conditions were deplorable, and Johnston reported that he had asked some 200 people how to get to Chattanooga before he finally happened upon the correct route. As you can tell, this was before the advent of billboards for Rock City and Ruby Falls, which would have simplified Johnston's task greatly.

The sudden prospect of visitors from the North being willing to shell out their hard-earned money just to tour the South proved to be the incentive needed to get government officials to take a second look at the condition of the region's highways. Immediately there arose

This postcard folder dates from the earliest days of Florida tourism.

Souvenir Folder of MIAMI BEACH Florida

A Public Bathing Beach

16M
PLACE
STAMP
HERE
100

a conflict between those interested in improving farm-to-market roads and those more concerned about the economic potential of establishing tourist routes. Money and power having the influence they do, the latter group won out.

The first two highways to be developed specifically to facilitate travel from the North to the South were the National Highway (1909) and the Capital Highway (1910). The National connected New York City with Atlanta; the Capital also ended in Atlanta, but received its name because its route began in Washington, D.C. and connected the state capitals of Richmond (Virginia), Raleigh (North Carolina), and Columbia (South Carolina).

Even though these two routes were unpaved over most of their length, the very fact that they had been established at all was a great improvement. Now Northerners could travel to at least parts of the South without getting lost on muddy, uncharted, back country roads, and the towns through which the National and the Capital passed soon found their business booming by virtue of the tourists now being brought directly to them. This did a marvelous job of catching the attention of the rest of the South.

In 1914, millionaire Carl Fisher, who had originally conceived Miami Beach with wealthy railroad passengers in mind, decided it was time to do something about opening his resort to automobile traffic as well. The result was the establishment the following year of the Dixie Highway, which began in Sault Sainte Marie, Michigan, and ended in Fisher's tropical wonderland. As it finally ran, the Dixie Highway actually consisted of both a western route and an eastern route. The two began and ended at the same points, but traversed completely different parts of the countryside in between.

The western path, after passing through the center of Indiana, entered the South at Louisville, Kentucky. En route to the Florida coast, it visited Nashville, Atlanta, Tallahassee, and

I Wish I Was in Dixie

5

Orlando. The eastern path came through Ohio, and its Southern locales included Lexington, Atlanta (where the two routes merged temporarily), Savannah, Jacksonville, and Daytona Beach. In addition, there was an extra Dixie Highway "spur" that took those who wished through North Carolina and the Great Smoky Mountains. The only way travelers could make sure they were still on their intended route was by the red-and-white "DH" signs that were posted along each of the highway's branches.

Two more major tourist routes were developed in the early 1920s. The Lee Highway, from New York to New Orleans, took travelers through Roanoke, Knoxville, Chattanooga, Birmingham, and Meridian. The Bankhead Highway, named for the Alabama senator who was an early booster for Southern highways, connected Washington, D.C. with San Diego by way of Charlotte, Atlanta, Birmingham, Memphis, and Little Rock. Other major routes developed in the early years of highway travel included the Jackson Highway (Chicago to New Orleans), the Jefferson Davis Highway (Washington, D.C. to San Francisco via the South), the Dixie Overland Highway (Savannah, Georgia, to Los Angeles), the Atlantic Coastal Highway (Quebec City, Canada, to Miami), and the Old Spanish Trail (San Diego to St. Augustine, Florida). Still more routes were developed within the individual states themselves: the

Tamiami Trail, connecting Tampa and Miami, and the Orange Blossom Trail, through central Florida's vast groves, for example.

By the mid-1920s, this profusion of named highways was getting to be more confusing than helpful. Routes overlapped frequently, and thus so did their trademark signposts along the roadsides. It was sometimes difficult to tell whether one was traveling the Dixie, Lee, Bankhead, or several of the above. The federal government determined to straighten out the mess by assigning uniform numbers to all of the nation's highways, clearly marking each with the now-classic white shield bearing the number of the highway.

The familiar pattern was set in November 1925. Highways running north and south were given odd numbers, while those running east and west were given even numbers. Primary highways were given single- or two-digit numbers, while those of lesser importance were given three-digit numbers. Now tourists found themselves faced with a whole new set of routes into the South. Some of the newly designated federal highways closely followed the paths of their named predecessors, while others struck out on their own, connecting together a number of local roads and other pathways to create a whole.

One of the primary north-south routes was U.S. 41, originating on the Canadian border at Copper Harbor, Michigan, and running all the way to Miami. This became the main highway for people traveling south from Chicago and the Midwest. U.S. 41 incorporated a large portion of the old Dixie Highway's western route, cutting through the very heart of the Southland and passing through Nashville, Chattanooga, Atlanta, and Tampa on its way to Florida's southernmost tip. (It would eventually become the first highway to feature advertising for Rock City Gardens.)

As the number assigned to it would suggest, U.S. 1 was another major route. This highway followed the South's eastern rim, passing through Richmond, Virginia and Raleigh, North Carolina, continuing on to the sights of the Okefenokee Swamp and down the Atlantic seaboard to Key West. Closely paralleling U.S. 1 in Florida was state highway A1A, which ran a little closer to the beaches and brought visitors to St. Augustine, Daytona Beach, and other nearby resorts. The northern part of U.S. 1 skirted New York City, so it was the logical route for that particular species of Yankee to take to visit their Southern neighbors.

U.S. 11, largely the old Lee Highway, took a radically different route. Running from Champlain (N.Y.), to New Orleans, it passed through the mountain country of Virginia and Tennessee, through Chattanooga (a crossing place for four or five Southern highways), on to Birmingham and Tuscaloosa (Ala.), and through the lower part of Mississippi. Advertising for Rock City, Sequoyah Caverns, Natural Bridge, and other famous attractions was comfortably entrenched on this route.

U.S. 25, from Port Austin (Mich.) to Brunswick (Ga.), was another latter-day portion of what was originally the eastern route of the Dixie Highway. During its heyday it gave birth to at least one later-famous Southern roadside institution. Passing through Kentucky, U.S. 25 made a national figure out of a local restaurateur, Harland Sanders, who was studying up new ways of frying chicken in his Corbin café. (The story of what became of Sanders and his delicious dish will be found in chapter 2.) Similar to U.S. 25 was U.S. 27, yet another route linking the frozen North with sunny Miami. It became another artery for Chattanooga and its Lookout Mountain attractions, and was one of the main feeding tubes for Silver Springs. In central Florida, U.S. 17 continued to be known as the Orange Blossom Trail, and passed through Orlando at a time when there was no sign of castles or talking mice in sight.

Other heavily traveled tourist highways included U.S. 31, from Michigan to Mobile (Ala.), with stops in Kentucky's cave country, Nashville, and Birmingham, where it passed beneath the feet of the giant Vulcan statue. In some areas it was known as "Bloody 31" because of its high number of accidents. U.S. 19 ran from Erie (Pa.), to St. Petersburg (Fla.), en route smoking a peace pipe with the Cherokee Indian reservation on the edge of the Great Smoky Mountains in North Carolina. The lifeline of the Smokies turned out to be U.S. 441, the main street of both Pigeon Forge and Gatlinburg, Tennessee. It went directly across the mountains to Cherokee, North Carolina before heading into Georgia and Florida. (U.S. 441 was nicknamed the "Uncle Remus Route," since one of its stops was Eatonton, Georgia, the birthplace of author Joel Chandler Harris.)

From the 1930s through the 1960s, road map covers were often breathtaking works of art.

Follow U. S. No. 27

The New Fast Arterial Highway
Thru SCENIC CENTRAL Florida

UNDERWATER AT
SILVER SPRINGS

FLOWERS OF CYPRESS GARDENS

BELLS OF BOK TOWER
THE NEW U.S. 27 HIGHWAY
IS THE SCENIC AND FAST ROUTE THRU
THE ORANGELAND OF CENTRAL FLORIDA
TO MIAMI VIA SILVER SPRINGS
CYPRESS GARDENS AND BOK TOWER
AND OTHER
WORLD FAMOUS TOURIST ATTRACTIONS.
FOLLOW U-S-27

All of the routes described above were obviously north-south roadways, as evidenced by their odd numbers. However, a few even-numbered east-west highways also made their mark on the South's attractions. U.S. 78, part of the old Bankhead Highway, connected Memphis (Tenn.) with the South Carolina coast, visiting Tupelo (Miss., later famed as the birthplace of Elvis You-Know-Who), Birmingham, and Atlanta, and making a destination out of Stone Mountain (Ga.). In Memphis, where 78 ran out, U.S. 70 took up the Bankhead's old path, running through Little Rock (Ark.), and down through the resort center of Hot Springs.

Both U.S. 280 and U.S. 431 (a north-south highway) were at one time designated as the "Florida Short Route," undoubtedly depending on whether one was traveling from the west or from the north. Their main influence on tourism came in Alabama, where U.S. 431 spawned the chain of Saxon's candy stores. While U.S. 280 was plowing from Birmingham toward the Georgia border, it passed through the rural farmlands of lower Alabama, where local businessman Fred Williams decided to construct his own tourist attraction. It became known as "The Bottle," because the combination service station and grocery store was built in the shape of a 64-foot-tall bottle of orange-flavored Nehi soft drink. The bottle cap served as an observation platform, reached via a staircase inside the building. Unfortunately, the wooden structure burned to the ground in 1933, but while it stood it was a terrific example of one of the earliest attractions built specifically for tourists on their way to the sunny and sandy beaches of Florida. Once the "Florida Short Route" travelers found themselves in that Sunshine State, they could choose U.S. 90 (the Old Spanish Trail), which began at Jacksonville and stretched west through Pensacola, Mobile, and the beaches of Biloxi, or U.S. 98, the famed "Miracle Strip" of Panama City Beach, Destin, Fort Walton Beach, and Pensacola Beach, with all of their goofy and exotic attractions.

In 1954, the *Chicago Tribune* set out to determine the best route for traveling from Chicago to Florida. They closely examined U.S. 41, the U.S. 31/280 "Florida Short Route," and the lesser-known U.S. 45, which sliced through Tennessee's western edge, through Memphis and the countryside of eastern Mississippi, ending in Mobile. (Presumably the tourists in question would then

THE SCENIC ROUTE
BETWEEN THE
MIDWEST AND FLORIDA

U.S. 25
U.S. 441

UNCLE
REMUS
ROUTE

THROUGH THE GREAT SMOKIES

"Highway of Southern Hospitality"

have chosen U.S. 90 to complete their trek.) The newspaper came to some definite conclusions about these three choices. It found that U.S. 45 was the safest route, owing to its relatively light traffic, but its condition deteriorated toward the end. "The last 50 miles into Mobile are on old, torturous pavement with blind curves and hill crests," the report went. U.S. 31/280 was the fastest, but featured long stretches with no towns, and hence no eating or sleeping facilities. U.S. 41, as might be expected, was judged the most interesting and most developed with tourism in mind, but the mountainous and sometimes foggy area around Chattanooga was prone to catch unwary flatlanders off guard.

No matter which route one chose, there were sure to be interesting sights to see along the way. Some of the best records of travel during this period are the postcards that were mailed to friends and family back home. Many individuals, of course, collect these postcards because of the attractions and businesses they depict, but it can be almost as fascinating to read people's firsthand reports on their trips-in-progress. One of the most informative was mailed from Morristown, Tennessee (a U.S. 11 stopover) to friends in Indiana on June 28, 1938: "Are on our way to Shenandoah Valley. Have covered 997 miles. Had a very nice cabin last night. Will stop and have a bite to eat at this burg. They sure do put out the eats down in this country. Yesterday we had three pieces of fried chicken . . . roast chicken, fried corn, dressing, salad, rolls, and iced tea for 35 cents."

Examples of the more leisurely pace of the time came from two other travelers, one of whom wrote from Roanoke, Virginia, on April 29, 1955: "Have had two days of beautiful driving through the Blue Ridge

GEORGIA'S STONE MOUNTAIN
JUST EAST OF ATLANTA ON U.S. 78

TRAVEL
US 70
COAST TO COAST
The Hospitality Route

CALIFORNIA
ARIZONA
NEW MEXICO
TEXAS

OKLAHOMA
ARKANSAS
TENNESSEE
NORTH CAROLINA

2926 MILES   ALL PAVED

"Route to Disneyland"

In the pre-Walt Disney World days, U.S. 70 was promoted as the "Route to Disneyland." It passed through three Southern states: North Carolina, Tennessee, and Arkansas.

10   I Wish I Was in Dixie

Mts. Will reach Washington today." The other mailed a message from Asheville, North Carolina, on June 13, 1950: "Never have I seen anything any more beautiful than the mountains entering Asheville. If the Smoky Mts. are any prettier we can't describe it. Don't know what we are going to do today. Don't know our route yet. But we'll be in the Smoky Mts. reservation sometime tomorrow." Oh, for those days when vacation time seemed to stretch out before one in an endless summer!

So, what about Florida? A series of postcards that were all mailed in December 1950 document a Pittsburgh couple's honeymoon trip through that colorful state. One card depicts Cordrey's Tourist Court in Ocala, and reads, "This is where we stayed last night. Yesterday we went to Bok Tower and Cypress Gardens, and through a fruit canning plant. Today we are going to visit Silver Springs." The saga continues on the next day's card, picturing Chandler's Tourist Court in Pensacola: "Arrived here about 9:15 from Silver Springs.

The drive today was beautiful, sunshine all the way. I hope it has stopped snowing in Pittsburgh." And at the bottom is the notation, "Rent, $5.00. Beautiful motel."

In 1949, a traveling couple visiting Panama City Beach reported, "Have a grand cottage with that wonderful breeze off the Gulf. We both hope you'll have our lawns mowed by the time we get home." A later (1957) report on Panama City Beach's development—which was just beginning to take off in earnest at the time—concerns the Long Beach Restaurant: "This place serves wonderful food. The only drawback: it is five miles from our motel, and the nearest restaurant at that. Our back door is only 20 feet from the water's edge." Just *try* to find five miles between a motel and restaurant on any of the Southern beaches today!

It is no accident that most of the recorded tourism history of this type dates from the mid-1930s on. The Great Depression did stunt the fledgling industry's growth to some extent, but between 1936 and 1941 tourists began returning to the highways. World War II and its gasoline and tire rationing again brought a halt to the flow; in later chapters we will see how various attractions and businesses had to cope with this four-year loss of trade. However, once the war was over an unprecedented boom in tourism hit, and continued unabated for more than twenty years.

By 1960, the South had well and truly become a force to be reckoned with in the tourism business. Any doubts about that were gone with the wind when the April 25, 1960, issue of *Life* magazine hit newsstands across the nation. There on the front cover, in all its stony splendor, was a special fold-out panoramic shot of Rock City Gardens' Lover's Leap, promoting an 18-page article describing great springtime vacation spots to be seen in the South.

In 1961 another national magazine, *Travel USA,* concocted a list of what they judged to be the top dozen tourist attractions in the country. Out of those twelve, seven were in the South: Colonial Williamsburg, Cypress Gardens, Luray Caverns, Rock City, Marineland of Florida, Mount Vernon, and Silver Springs. As many post-Civil War optimists had predicted, the South had indeed risen again!

In the days of the old two-lane federal highways, "individuality" was the key word in describing the roadside landscape. With the exception of such giants as the chain of Howard Johnson's restaurants, corporate America did not heavily intrude upon private enterprise along the older highways. Restaurants, motels, and even attractions themselves were owned by individual families, some of whom kept and maintained their businesses for several generations. This individuality extended into the advertising that could be found along the highways, often manifesting itself in ways that would have horrified a professional ad agency. Painted barn roofs were the prime example of this folksy form of advertising, as made famous by Rock City, Sequoyah Caverns, North Carolina's chain of Sterchi furniture stores, and many others. Since roadside signs were made and erected with no regulations to restrict

The makers of this salt water taffy employed every possible Florida emblem.

Hillbilly, bear, and Indian images decorated taffy boxes in the Great Smoky Mountains.

SMOKY MOUNTAIN
TAFFY LOGS
TRADE MARK
PURE WHOLESOME CANDY

SMOKY MOUNTAIN TAFFY

NET WT.

them, it was not uncommon to find advertisements for businesses beginning several hundred miles ahead of time.

(This phenomenon became so common that it even inspired a comedy bit on the *I Love Lucy* TV show in 1955. Driving cross country, Lucy, Ricky, Fred, and Ethel encounter 500 miles of signs advertising "Aunt Sally's Pecans & Pralines." When they finally arrive, they find the candy shop closed and out of business. Fred remarks, "I thought Aunt Sally was spending too much money on all those signs.")

The success enjoyed by the entrepreneurs who thrived by the side of the road did not go unnoticed by state tourism departments. With their years of experience in dealing with out-of-

state traffic, it is not surprising that Florida was the first to elect for extending a more personal greeting to their throngs of visitors. In November 1949, the first state-operated "Welcome Station," an amazingly new idea, was opened at the Florida state line on U.S. 17. More stations were added in the years between 1952 and 1954, until eventually one could be found at the Florida border on all the main tourist routes.

At the new Florida Welcome Stations, tourists could refresh themselves with complimentary glasses of genuine Florida orange juice and pick up brochures and other advertising for the state's attractions and accommodations. The basic idea started to catch on in other locales as well.

the tourism industry. Now, though, something was about to take place that would shake that industry to its very asphalt. It was called the Interstate Highway System.

During World War II, General Dwight Eisenhower had been greatly impressed with the highway system in Germany. The Autobahn, as their network was called, was a vast improvement over the American highway system, which in the mid-1950s was still carrying millions of travelers over routes that had been set in 1925. Once Eisenhower became President of the United States, he set about bringing the nation's roads up to date. This led to the creation of the Federal Interstate Highway Department in 1956.

In 1961, the first non-Florida welcome center opened on U.S. 301 in Georgia; appropriately, the Georgia welcome centers served free peanuts and Coca-Cola (whose home base was Atlanta). Within a few years, each state in the South had opened its own centers, and the concept was here to stay.

However, it was around this same time that the winds of change began to whisper in the palm trees of Florida and the pines of the Great Smokies. When the automobile and the highway had replaced the locomotive and the railroad as the primary form of long-distance travel, that had meant major adjustments for

The Florida Welcome Stations were an innovation when the first one opened in 1949.

Many towns, businesses, and tourist attractions were thrown into a frenzy by the announcement of the government's new plan. The interstate highways would not follow the routes of the older highways, but would strike out across the countryside, bypassing small towns and allowing drivers to exit only at certain predetermined points. Granted, everyone agreed that this ability to handle more traffic via a safer method than the old two-lanes (where a careless driver was apt to pull out in front of one at any moment) was a great idea, but what was going to become of the businesspeople who had staked their very lives on old U.S. 41, U.S. 1, and their like?

It took the interstate system some fifteen years or so to replace most of the old federal highways in the South. But as more highways were bypassed, a drastic change took place in what tourists were able to see during their long journeys. For all of their advantages, probably the biggest thing that was lost during the switch from highways to interstates was the sense of place. Because the interstates generally ran so far from any sort of human development, it was often difficult to tell one state from another. Scores of mom-and-pop motels and restaurants along the old highways were unable to survive in the face of competition from slick chain establishments much more conveniently located at interstate exits.

For "roadside" attractions the situation was just as bad, and their classification was now inaccurate. Now that great numbers of tourists no longer passed directly by their entrance gates every day, the attractions had to concentrate on convincing people that it was worth time and effort to exit from the interstate and drive several miles to visit them. Most of them

planned on doing this by plastering the new routes with directional billboards pointing the way to their wonders. But that would soon prove to be more difficult than they ever imagined.

Along with the institution of the interstate system came a new public concern for preserving the beauty of the natural landscape. When the program was first announced, it was stated that these new routes would enable drivers to see more of the countryside, *uncluttered by roadside advertising*. If the loss of the old highway traffic sent the tourism industry into fits, this announcement was enough to cause panic in the streets. For many roadside businesses, billboards and other signs were their only form of advertising at all. Removal of this option would be the death sentence.

The fight for highway beautification had been going on since the invention of the automobile, but it reached a fever pitch during the early 1960s. By then, the postwar tourism boom had created a veritable forest of advertising lining every major tourist route. In 1961, a Knoxville, Tennessee, newspaper decided to do an in-depth survey on the roadside blight in the region around the Great Smoky Mountains, nicknamed "Billboard Alley." The reporter documented that for almost an hour she had been told "where to go, what bread to take home, urged to use the paint that stretches, and menacingly informed to stay at some luxurious abobe because I'm sleepy." She remarked that she had never visited Rock City or Ft. Weare Game Park (an early Pigeon Forge attraction), but had always wanted to do so . . . until she grew tired of their incessant roadside advertising.

Of course, there are two sides to every argument, even this one. Indeed, in some areas the billboards and signs were crowded so closely together that they cancelled one another out, not to mention obscuring the surrounding scenery. But, as another writer pointed out, there were many areas of the South that had beautiful scenery, but were still economically depressed because of a lack of commercial businesses . . . and businesses had to be able to advertise their presence along the highways. The public itself seemed split on the issue: for everyone who deplored the commercialization of the roadside scene, there was someone else who actually enjoyed reading the signs and

counting down the miles to the next wonder spot.

When first John F. Kennedy and, later, Lady Bird Johnson threw their influence behind the highway beautification program, the result was sweeping alterations in the familiar roadside environment. A compromise was reached: some advertising would be allowed along the new interstates, but only in certain areas, and under various restrictions. Signs now had to be licensed, so the hundreds of miles of billboards promoting one small business vanished. The chain of Stuckey's candy stores was adversely affected by this, too. Even on the older highways, new regulations were put into effect, causing Rock City to paint over many of its barn roofs and drastically reducing the number of advertisements that could be seen through the windshield.

Although they were few, there were those who took the time to notice that an era in tourism history had drawn to a close. In 1973, Maxine Thompson, a writer for *Georgia* magazine, penned

South of the Border, a roadside stop on U.S. 301 at Dillon, South Carolina, was one of the most aggressive billboard advertisers in the South.

I Wish I Was in Dixie

The elimination of sign clutter, such as this jumble at the base of Lookout Mountain, was one of the main objectives of Lady Bird Johnson's 1965 Highway Beautification Act.

an eloquent tribute to the old, bypassed highways. It read in part:

With the furor being raised about giant billboards all but wiping out the scenery along our highways, especially the newer interstate routes, a ride along one of the older roads shows that the advertising agents of grandpa's day did a pretty good job of using what they found available.

Along on U.S. Highway 41, for example, which slices through Georgia from north to south, messages on barn tops, barn sides, and even dilapidated cabins-turned-barns still shout at the passerby to SEE ROCK CITY, SEE SEVEN STATES FROM LOOKOUT MOUNTAIN, and SEE RAINBOW SPRINGS in giant letters.

It doesn't pay to ride along this or some of the other older roads in the state while you're hungry. Hand-painted signs nailed to trees regale you with promises of "Fresh Peaches," "Country Hams," "Pecan Candies," or "Pit Bar-B-Q," along with souvenirs and gifts. They start giving the distance in miles, then in hundreds of feet, and finally in feet, until the drooling driver is led almost by the hand to a roadside stand loaded with fresh fruit, or perhaps a closed and boarded-up old building that represents a once-thriving business killed by the new interstate highway a few miles away.

Unlike the sheared-clean expressways, though, these older roads treat the tourist to the near-forgotten sight and smell of Seven Sisters roses spilling over a sagging fence or the heavenly perfume of a tall, dew-drenched cape jasmine nestled against the corner of a deserted shack. Gnarled chinaberry trees that once played host to a generation of boys and tomboys who swarmed over their limbs now seem to droop their umbrella-shaped branches in loneliness. A solitary chimney, all that is left of a home that heard the ring of laughter and saw the tears of sorrow, is decorated with swirls of kudzu vines and a brick company advertisement.

Don't ride over one of these roads when you're in a hurry. Take time to browse, to read the faded old signs on the barns. One of these days the last one of them will complete its crumble into decay. When that happens, a segment of history will fade away.

Fading away it was indeed, but the interstates were not the only cause. In 1965, an announcement had been made that was going to have a permanent effect on the way people thought of vacationing in the South. Late that year, the legendary Walt Disney confirmed circulating rumors that he had purchased several thousand acres of swampland near Orlando, in central Florida, and he and his company would be opening a multimillion-dollar complex to be known as Disney World.

Walt Disney died in 1966, the year after making his much-anticipated announcement, and he never got to see the completion of his biggest project. It finally opened in October 1971, Walt's brother Roy having officially renamed the complex "*Walt* Disney World" so everyone would know exactly whose idea it had been.

At least at first, the other Southern attractions welcomed the arrival of Disney with celebration, as they realized what an increase in tourists it was going to produce. But with increased numbers came still more problems.

Suddenly, venerable places like Silver Springs found themselves no longer being considered as vacation destinations, but rather as places people stopped off at while on their way to Disney's land. Attractions immediately began adding to their advertising such phrases as "Only one hour from Disney World." In other words, once Mickey Mouse came to town, everyone else became just an afterthought. One former motel owner from southern Florida made the statement that when the gargantuan theme park made its appearance, "it was as if someone had built a wall across the middle of the state," preventing tourists from venturing any further south than Orlando. Perhaps this problem was more keenly felt in Florida itself than in the other Southern states, but all of the region's attractions eventually found themselves being compared to the magic of the Disney kingdom.

And so, with the opening of Walt Disney World, the history of Southern tourism entered its present-day phase. What does the future hold? It is as impossible to predict as it would have been in 1888, 1925, 1947, or any other year. But it is possible to look back and see what has gone before. Turn the page, and begin to sample the incredible variety that made up Dixie . . . before Disney.

Stuckey's, Ten Miles

Thank God the North won the war. It would have been awful if there hadn't been any Yankees to sell to.

—Williamson Sylvester Stuckey

The following scene is one that could have taken place anywhere in the United States: a family is about to set out on their annual summer vacation trip, and most likely the drive will take at least a couple of days. Once that car pulls out of its comfortable suburban driveway, there are certain needs that are going to have to be met before it reaches its destination. Gasoline is vital to keep the vehicle running, of course, but these being the pre-liberated days, it is primarily the responsibility of dear ol' Dad to keep an eye on the gas gauge and decide which gleaming service station will best suit him. For the rest of the human inhabitants of the conveyance, eating and sleeping are the two main concerns (ranking right up there with "I gotta go to the bathroom," "How many more miles?" and "Are we there yet?").

Fortunately for our hypothetical family, the Southern highways were far from devoid of establishments to serve all these needs. One that seemed to be ubiquitous south of the Mason-Dixon line was heralded by huge, flaming yellow billboards with red letters reading, in an unmistakable script logo, "Stuckey's."

Of all the restaurants, motels, souvenir shops, and service stations that could be found along the highways, Stuckey's most definitively spelled "the South" to travelers from other parts of the country. Even in later years, when the chain had spread all the way to the West Coast and as far north as Minnesota, many tourists felt that they had truly entered the South when they saw Stuckey's famous signs. Such a reputation as a Southern roadside fixture was well-deserved and hard-earned.

It all started back in the dark Depression days of the early 1930s. Twenty-one-year-old Williamson Sylvester Stuckey had been attending college at the University of Georgia when family funds ran out in 1931. He returned home to his family's cotton farm in Eastman, Georgia, to try to help out, but the Depression soon killed the cotton market as surely as it had the stock market. Stuckey was forced to seek employment elsewhere.

In an interview later in life, Stuckey recalled: "I went to a warehouseman and asked him for a job. He didn't have anything. He said he could give me a job, but he couldn't pay me. He told me I ought to go into the pecan business. He said, 'You've got a Ford coupe. Drive it around and buy pecans and sell 'em." W. S. Stuckey entered the pecan business with $35.00 and two sacks containing a mixed variety of pecans. "I would buy pecans after 3:00 when the bank closed so I could write checks; then I would sell enough to deposit the money the next morning to cover the checks."

The turning point in this nutty way of life came when Stuckey erected a small wooden stand by the side of the road. Fortunately, East-man was located on both U.S. 23 and U.S. 341, two of the many routes used by travelers on their way to Florida. At first the tourists were satisfied with the bags of pecans they could buy at this first Stuckey's location, but then a new twist caused business to pick up faster than the Stuckeys' pecan pickers could pluck pecans.

"My wife Ethel started cooking chocolate fudge," Stuckey recalled. "Then maple divinity and pralines. A nurse for our children lived on the farm with us, and my wife taught her how to cook the candy too." When candy—especially pecan candy—was added to the inventory, the tourists went nuts.

As the operation grew, Stuckey decided it would be a good idea to expand his territory. First he replaced the wooden stand with a more

substantial building just south of East-man; then he began casting about for other likely locations. By 1941, a second Stuckey's had opened on U.S. 41 at Unadilla, Georgia, and a third at the point where U.S. 1 crossed the state line into Florida.

As with the rest of the tourism industry, Stuckey's was practically struck out by World War II. During the days of tire and gasoline rationing, tourists were no longer hitting the road. That was probably just as well, because the government's sugar rationing would have made it practically impossible for production of Stuckey's candies to continue anyway. All locations but the original Eastman store closed up for the duration, but W. S. Stuckey managed to stay in the black by producing candy for the armed forces, which enabled him to get at least a certain allotment of sugar for his goodies.

Everyone in the tourist business breathed a sigh of relief when the war ended in 1945. Little did they know just what a huge boom was about to hit the industry, but Stuckey's was

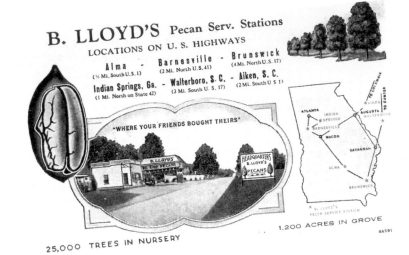

The ancestor of Stuckey's and all of its successors was B. Lloyd's Pecan Service Stations, seen here in this 1934 postcard.

This magazine ad dates from 1952, when Stuckey's was just beginning to spread along the roadsides throughout the South.

right there leading the charge. The original Stuckey stores reawakened after their wartime slumber, and were soon joined by more and more locations in the chain. "Co-branding," a popular term in the business world today, was practically originated by Stuckey's, which has enjoyed an association with Texaco for its gasoline pumps since the late 1940s, and in more recent years hooked up with fast food chain Dairy Queen.

The 1950s and 1960s were Stuckey's golden period. Besides the ever-popular pecan candy, the stores grew to include snack bars and large, well-stocked souvenir shops. There was a certain logic to the locations of these shops and the selection of merchandise they sold. Bill Stuckey Jr., who now heads the company, explains that most Stuckey's stores were located on the right-hand side of the highways as people returned *home* from Florida. The reason behind this was simple. On their way *to* Florida, economy-minded tourists were more likely to be watching their wallets closely, and besides, they really didn't want to lug sacks full of knick-knacks around with them throughout their whole two-week vacation. But coming home, it was a different pair of pecans altogether. People whose trips were nearly over were better prospects for buying unnecessary things like seashell lamps and rubber alligators, thus explaining why a Stuckey's store in, say, Alabama or Tennessee would be found selling souvenirs from any of the neighboring states from which customers might be returning.

Stuckey's had always done well on the old original federal highways, but it was the coming of the interstates that made it a true giant in the roadside world. W. S. Stuckey pioneered the business of operating at interstate exits, at a time when such companies as McDonald's and Burger King were not even thinking of such tactics. Stuckey developed a method for choosing his locations that was unique to say the least. He would set out from a given spot—Atlanta, for instance—and he would drive along the interstate until he felt the urge to visit a restroom. Wherever that familiar need struck him would be the next location for a Stuckey's store. Sound odd? Perhaps to a mar-

Stop at Stuckey's... buy 10 gallons of gas and get a box of **free candy**

Your happiest stop on the highways! Relax, refresh, refuel at Stuckey's. Find every service that makes motoring easier and more fun.

Enjoy good food at our fast snack bars; golden fried chicken. Great pecan candies, gift packs (we mail for you anywhere). Gas up with ten or more gallons and a box of our fine candy is yours free. Texaco, Diners Club, American Express for any purchase. Coast to coast—every trip's a pleasure trip when you stop at Stuckey's.

Stuckey's STUCKEY STORES DIVISION PET INCORPORATED

keting expert, but no one could argue with the success of this rationale. During the 1960s, a Stuckey's store was like an oasis in the desert of the interstates' long, barren stretches.

For most of this period, Stuckey's was actually operating as a division of the giant Pet Milk Company, of which W. S. Stuckey was made a vice president. Now Stuckey's made a concentrated attempt to give its stores a more eye-catching roadside look. For many years, the Stuckey's buildings were nothing distinctive in themselves; quite often, the Stuckey's logo and products were simply grafted onto existing buildings. All of that changed under Pet's direction. In the 1960s the buildings began to be roofed with shiny teal-colored enamel tile, which made them easily identifiable from a distance. Around 1970 a new building was introduced, topped with what was officially known as the "cathedral" roof. These huge, swooping designs became intimately associated with Stuckey's, although in the days of spiraling energy costs they became more of a liability than an asset. At many locations, the magnificent

During Stuckey's years of ownership by Pet, promotions took many forms, including this board game and offer of free candy.

exposed Canadian wood of the cathedral roofs' interiors was sealed off by inexpensive drop ceilings. (Fortunately, today at least some of the stores are making a conscious effort to restore their original cathedral ceilings.)

According to Bill Stuckey Jr., the popularity of Stuckey's peaked in the early 1970s, when the chain comprised some 330 stores in 44 states. Then the 1973–74 energy crunch thinned the ranks of potential tourists almost as badly as World War II had, and Stuckey's was obliged to change with the times. The days when families would set out from New York and drive all the way to Florida, stopping at Stuckey's going in both directions, became a thing of the past. Deregulation of the airlines caused fares to plummet, making it much more economical (and quicker) for people to *fly* to their vacation destinations. Almost half of the peak number of Stuckey's stores were forced to close. Today the chain stands at around 150 shops.

The large number of abandoned Stuckey's stores caused further changes for the company. Because of their distinctive design, the brightly-colored cathedral roofs made even a deserted Stuckey's hard to disguise. "These buildings were everything but Stuckey's," Bill Jr. says. "They were everything from strip joints to shell shops, and we had to find some way to enable the public to distinguish an operating Stuckey's from a closed Stuckey's." Bill Jr.'s

solution was to repaint the roofs on the still-operating stores. Instead of teal, a deep blue color was used, and this was even extended to the famous yellow and red signs. The lettering remained red, with a yellow outline just to remind people of the old days, but the backgrounds became the same blue color used on the roofs. In 1997, the chain truly made a switch back to its origins when the signage on the buildings and billboards reverted to the long-standing red-against-yellow color scheme.

W. S. Stuckey Sr. passed away in 1977, but the company he founded, while somewhat smaller than in its peak years, is still an integral part of the American roadside scene. Stuckey's has always seemed most at home in the South, and continues to be a welcome sight for any travelers looking for a place to grab a quick bite or a classic-style souvenir.

Stuckey's was undoubtedly the king of the Southern roadside "candy shoppes," but it was not alone. During the wartime days when Stuckey's was producing candy for American servicemen, a fellow by the name of Bob Horne came to work for the company. Horne also ran a tourist court on U.S. 1 at Bayard, Florida, just outside Jacksonville. Sometime in the early 1950s, Horne got the idea to open his own candy and gift shop at his tourist court, and it was successful enough that he was soon able to build an even larger store nearby.

Stuckey's chief competitor, Horne's, began with this shop on U.S. 1 at Bayard, Fla.

Horne's really horned in on Stuckey's during the 1960s. Although it never developed as large a place in the public consciousness as Stuckey's had, Horne's easily ran second when it came to the total number of locations. Their buildings were shaped something like a hybrid of Stuckey's and Howard Johnson's, but it was their roofs that gave them their most distinctive feature. When Stuckey's began flashing their loud teal-colored roofs at travelers' eyes, Horne's countered with blindingly shiny yellow rooftop tiles that no one could possibly

miss. (Even today, many of the abandoned Horne's locations still sport their yellow roofs, which have not faded in the least over the years.) Surprisingly, considering their heated rivalry in business, according to Bill Stuckey Jr. the Horne and Stuckey families remained close friends for years.

Horne's thrived throughout the 1960s and into the early 1970s, but once the real heyday of highway travel had passed, they quickly dropped out of sight. Unlike Stuckey's, Horne's went into the motel business in a big way

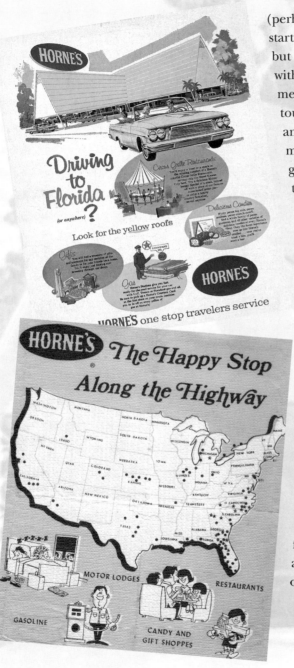

(perhaps due to the fact that they started as part of a tourist court), but those too were unable to cope with a changing roadside environment. The original Horne's tourist court in Bayard became an antique shop, and today many people have totally forgotten about what was once the heir apparent to Stuckey's candy-coated throne.

Stuckey's and Horne's may have been the two biggest contenders for the Southern traveler's sweet tooth, but they were not the only ones. For nearly thirty years, tourists also flocked to another home-grown chain, Saxon's. The Saxon's story begins in 1939, when salesman Henry E. Saxon and his wife Cora were living in Birmingham, Alabama. They had fallen in love with the product of a local candymaker, Pop Kavenaugh, who had made quite a reputation for himself in the Birmingham area. Mrs. Saxon recalls that one night, while enjoying some

of Kavenaugh's product after dinner, Henry remarked that if one could learn how to make candy of that quality and market it over a widespread area, the resulting money would be scrumptious.

"Nothing else was said about it," Mrs. Saxon says, "and Henry went into the living room to read the newspaper while I finished clearing the dinner table. A few minutes later he rushed back into the kitchen, all excited and waving the newspaper. That very day, Pop Kavenaugh had put an ad in the paper saying that he was about to retire, and that he would teach his candy recipes to only *two* people before he quit."

It doesn't take an MBA to figure out which two people were accepted to inherit the Kavenaugh formula, but originally the Saxons gave no thought to the possibility of attracting highway tourists with their sweet wares. For nearly a decade (interrupted by World War II, of course) the Saxon brand of candy was sold strictly in local stores and through a booming mail order business, not out on the open roads.

By 1947 Saxon's candies had become successful enough that the couple built their first roadside stand, nicknamed the "Candy Box," at Wellington, Alabama, on U.S. 431 (one of several "Florida Short Routes"). It became a popular spot not only for the local trade, but for the travelers who were cutting through that part of the state on their way to the beaches. Before long, Mrs. Saxon says, "the candy was selling faster than we could make it." In 1953, Saxon's finally became a full-fledged chain of candy and gift shops. Following the format established by Stuckey's and Horne's, the Saxons added restaurants to their stores in 1955.

Over the years, approximately forty Saxon's locations operated in Alabama, Georgia, Tennessee, and Florida. Unlike their bigger competitors, the Saxon's chain never developed one uniform building style that was used for every location. During the 1960s, when Stuckey's teal roofs and Horne's yellow ones were brightening the roadside scene, many (but not all) of the Saxon's stores featured loud red roofs. Saxon's most identifiable trademark turned out to be their roadside sign, a giant candy cane. More than twenty feet tall, the signs were neon spectaculars yummy enough to drag drooling travelers off the highway even if they were unfamiliar with the chain itself.

Cora Saxon's expertise had always been in the physical manufacturing of the candy itself, while the day-to-day business of managing a chain of stores was left up to her husband. After Henry Saxon's untimely death in an automobile accident in November 1968, Mrs. Saxon allowed their shops to gradually go out of business as the leases on the buildings expired.

Saxon's packaging mined its Deep South image for all it was worth, much to customers' delight.

However, the Saxon's brand of candy remained on sale in independent gift shops across the South. Mismanagement by Henry Saxon's successors, combined with the escalating cost of the quality ingredients Mrs. Saxon insisted on using, caused the complete discontinuation of the company in the late 1970s.

Undoubtedly, the Southern roadside business scene was most closely identified with these three chains of candy shops. However, some of today's largest international corporations began their histories as nothing more than individual entities built to serve tourists who just happened to be passing their way. The classic example of this situation could be found in Corbin, Kentucky.

Now, Corbin was hardly the tourist capital of the South. It featured no attractions, no beaches, no Great Smoky Mountains. Nevertheless, in 1930 it was the town chosen by a small-time businessman and amateur cook, Harland Sanders, as a desirable place to open a service station. Always looking for ways to increase business, Sanders wheeled his family's dining table into a 15 × 15-foot room in his service station, and began cooking dinners for travelers on U.S. 25. "We'd cook for the five of us and have it ready at 11:00 or thereabouts," he later recalled. "This way we was ready for the people comin' from the North who was on Eastern time."

The tiny café, such as it was, made such a hit that when Sanders bought out his competition and moved to a better location across the street, he included a full-fledged restaurant in his new building. Sanders speculated that the fact he was located at a major intersection had a lot to do with his ever-increasing business: "I was at the fork of the roads where U.S. 25E went to Asheville down through the Smoky Mountains. Route 25W took them through Knoxville and on down to Atlanta."

Sanders' Café became such a popular stopping place that in 1935 Kentucky governor Ruby Lafoon (yes, that was his name) conferred upon Sanders the honorary title of Kentucky Colonel. (Now you know where this story is heading, if you hadn't already figured it out.) Within a couple of years he was able to construct a motel on a vacant lot adjoining his restaurant and service station, so tourists could now obtain their three basic needs—gas, food, and lodging—all in one spot. In fact, Sanders even came up with the novel idea of constructing a model of one of his motel rooms right in the middle of his restaurant, so persnickety wives could inspect it before deciding whether to spend the night.

In chapter 1 we saw how the rise of the interstate highway system brought both good and bad times to Southern tourism. So it was with Sanders' Court and Café. When Interstate 75 replaced old U.S. 25, routing traffic miles away from Corbin, Sanders had no choice but to sell his motel, service station, and restaurant at auction in 1956. The price he got for it barely paid his taxes and outstanding bills. It looked like it was the end of the road for the aging Kentucky Colonel.

Well, you probably know the rest of the story. With great confidence in the recipe he

Harland Sanders first developed his special recipe for fried chicken at this motel on U.S. 25 in Corbin, Kentucky.

had developed for frying chicken in his café, Sanders donned a white suit, mustache, and goatee, became known as Colonel Sanders, and set out to franchise his "Kentucky" fried chicken to restaurants across the country. For years, Kentucky Fried Chicken was available only as a menu item at scores of drive-ins and restaurants, until in the mid-1960s the corporation began building its own candy-striped stand-alone stores.

But what about the original Sanders' Court in Corbin? Its fortunes bounced up and down for more than a decade, until the property was purchased by the Kentucky Fried Chicken corporation in 1969. They promptly demolished the motel and service station, but continued to operate the restaurant as one of their own outlets. Finally, in 1990 Sanders' Café was meticulously restored to its original (circa 1939) appearance, even including the recreation of the model motel room. Now not only was KFC's future assured, but so was its past!

Fried chicken being a traditionally Southern delicacy, it is not surprising that Colonel Sanders's success caused the region to become the incubator for a coop full of competitors, most of whom tried to latch on to some sort of unique selling point to distinguish themselves from all the others. Nashville-based Minnie Pearl's Fried Chicken was endorsed by the

Colonel Sanders's Kentucky Fried Chicken began as a menu item in independent restaurants, such as this North Carolina drive-in.

This menu dates from Kentucky Fried Chicken's drive-in days.

raucous Grand Ole Opry comedienne herself. There was Yogi Bear's Honey Fried Chicken, which thought it was better than the average chicken, and brought Hanna-Barbera's jovial buffoon to the roadside in the form of a gigantic illuminated sign. Appropriately enough, New Orleans-based Popeye's Famous Fried Chicken first muscled its way into cities along the Gulf coast before gradually working inland.

Meanwhile, Bojangles Fried Chicken danced out of Charlotte, North Carolina.

Fried chicken outlets were not the only chain restaurants to begin in Dixie. Seafood server Long John Silver's set sail from the famous old seaport of Lexington, Kentucky, while the harbor at Nashville brought forth Captain D's (originally called *Mr. D's*), and Red Lobster crawled out of Lakeland, Florida. Several hamburger chains were also ground out of the South. Krystal's sparkling white buildings and tiny square burgers, inspired by the Midwest's White Castle chain, made their first appearance in Chattanooga in 1932. Burger King, the omnipresent pain in Ronald McDonald's neck, first began establishing its regime on Beach Boulevard in Jacksonville, Florida, in 1953. Yet another burger baron, Hardee's, was born in Greenville, North Carolina, in 1961, and its "charco-broiled" hamburgers were soon burning up the roads. Lum's, with its famous "hot dogs steamed in beer," staggered out of Miami in 1957. Within a decade Lum's had spread all over the country and to several foreign lands as well.

The remaining business that catered to tourists—motels—also got a boost from the South. In 1951, Memphis builder Kemmons Wilson noticed something strange: "I had five children," he recalled, "and when we went on our vacations, suddenly my eight dollar room became eighteen dollars. I told my wife that this was unfair, because nobody would want to travel with their children." What did Wilson propose to do about it? He had an idea: "I said, 'I'm going home and I'm going to build a chain of motels across the country, and I'll never make a charge for children as long as they live in the same room as their parents. I also wanted to have a clean room, with a television. My motel was going to have everything I wanted myself.'"

Wilson enlisted the aid of a Memphis architect, who drew up plans for the new business according to its originator's instructions. "Four or five days later he came back with the drawing," said Wilson, "and up at the top he had scratched the name HOLIDAY INN. I said, 'That's a pretty good name, where'd you get it?' He said, 'I saw Bing Crosby in that movie on television last night.' I said, 'That's a great name; we'll use it!'"

Kemmons Wilson's Holiday Inn Hotel Court opened on August 2, 1952, on Memphis's Summer Avenue, which did triple duty as U.S. 64, U.S. 70, and U.S. 79. The eventual dominance of this franchised chain can be largely attributed to the consistency of the service provided at all of its locations, much like the appeal of chain-oriented fast food. There was certainly nothing particularly distinctive about the physical appearance of the Holiday Inn motels themselves. For a time, Holiday Inn heavily promoted its own trademark character, a fictional colonial innkeeper named John Holiday, but even the presence of his life-sized statue in the motel lobbies was not the chain's primary claim to fame. Instead, the emblem that immediately made all of them stand out from the surrounding cityscape was their self-dubbed "Great Sign."

Trademark historian Hal Morgan reports that the classic Holiday Inn sign was some 43 feet tall, with 836 feet of neon tubing and 426 incandescent bulbs. Glowing and pulsating in a psychedelic array of white, green, orange, red, blue, yellow, and pink, it became a welcome nighttime sight for a generation of weary travelers. But the signs' construction cost of $35,000 each, coupled with $3,700 electric bills and $2,400 maintenance costs for each one, eventually doomed their existence. In the early 1980s the Great Signs were gradually dismantled and replaced with rather dull green backlit plastic signs. The famous star that radiated from the topmost point of the Great Sign was reduced to an abstract emblem on the new Holiday Inn logo.

Despite the eventual preponderance of the huge chain motels, most people's memories of traveling in the South revolve more around the independent, or what have become known as the "mom-and-pop," motels. These were the

The first Holiday Inn opened on Summer Avenue in Memphis, Tennessee, in 1952.

Holiday Inn's "Great Sign" became a welcome nighttime sight to generations of weary travelers.

backbone of the South's tourist industry for many years before Holiday Inn's flashing signs, and they continued to be a viable roadside presence right up to the time when the interstate system replaced the old federal highways.

Actually, the meaning of the term "motel" became somewhat corrupted once it reached the Southern quarter of the country. The word, a contraction of "motor hotel," originated in California in 1925, and referred to lodging that consisted of several connected rooms under one roof. Previously, various terms such as "motor court" and "tourist court" had been used to designate the standard groupings of individual cottages that were the most common rest stops prior to World War II. The word "motel" remained West Coast terminology for many years: in 1940, the only business in the South to be designated by that name was Quail's Motel in Fort Smith, Arkansas. Once the phrase caught on after the war, groups of tourist cabins suddenly took on the "motel" name, while some motels continued to use the term "court" or "tourist court." For the sake of simplicity, here we are using the term "motel" to describe any of them.

One of the most charming things about these independent motels was the way they frequently attempted to connect themselves with the area they served, either through their architecture or, more often, through their names and amazingly creative signage. As might be expected, in the beach areas motels were keen on conjuring up images of sand and surf. For example, there was the Sea Breeze Hotel, Gulf Crest

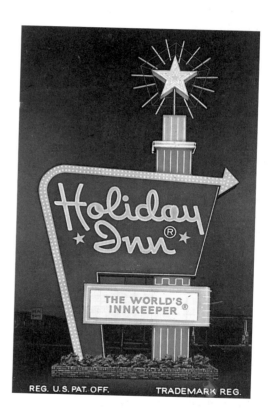

LOUISVILLE, KY.

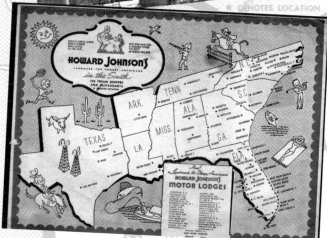

Howard Johnson's was one of the first national restaurant chains to establish a presence along the Southern roadside.

Beach, Fla.), the Gulf Breeze Inn (Gulf Shores, Ala.), Gulf Palms Hotel Court (Pass Christian, Miss.), the Silver Beach Hotel (Fort Walton Beach, Fla.), the Sea Gull Tourist Court and the Sun-N-Sand Motel (Biloxi, Miss.), the Sea Spray Cottage Court (Jacksonville Beach, Fla.), and the Flamingo Motel (Ocala, Fla.).

Others went for the tropical approach, trying for connections with South Seas imagery: the Palm Plaza (Winter Park, Fla.), Palms Court (Waycross, Ga.), the Palmetto Court, Tropical Breeze Motel, and Reef Motel (Panama City Beach), Islander Motel (Fort Walton Beach), Trade Winds Hotel Court (Biloxi), and Tropical Palms Court (Daytona Beach, Fla.). Then there was the case of the Ocean Pines Court in Myrtle Beach, South Carolina: how many people think of "ocean" and "pines" in the same sentence?

In the mountains, motels followed a different pattern. References to the Great Smoky Mountains popped up most often, as in the Smokyland Motel and Smoky Mtn. Plaza (both in Gatlinburg, Tenn.), and the Highland Tourist Court and Smoky Mt. Tourist Court (both in Knoxville, Tenn.). Running a close second were references to the region's familiar bears: Gatlinburg's Bearskin Cottages, Bearland Motel, and Sleepy Bear Motel, and

Motel, Fun-N-Sand Motel, Sun-N-Swim Motel, Sea Sand Motel, White Sands Motel, Beacon Motel, and Sandpiper Motel (all in Panama City

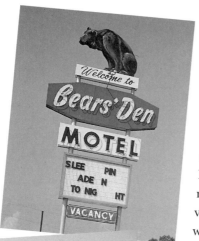

Bears were the preferred logo for businesses in the Great Smoky Mountains.

the Smoky Cub Motor Court and Smoky Bear Motel (Sevierville, Tenn.). Hillbilly stereotypes were deployed at the Mountaineer Motel (Gatlinburg) and the Hillbilly Hilton (Townsend, Tenn.). Not surprisingly, Cherokee, North Carolina, capitalized on its Indian heritage with the Wigwam Motel, Thunderbird Motel, and Chief Motel. Lookout Mountain's rocky slopes were heavy with motels bearing the peak's name or some variation thereof. Also to be found there was the Fairyland Court, named after the residential development created by Rock City founder Garnet Carter (and, one suspects, Rock City's nearby Fairyland Caverns).

Some motels chose to identify themselves with the U.S. highways they served: the A1A Court (St. Augustine, Fla.), 78 Motel (Birmingham, Ala.), and 301 Motor Court (Glennville, Ga.) are examples of this line of thinking. Others went after identification with the South in general: the Dixie Inn (Panama City Beach), Old South Motel (Atlanta), Dixieland Motel (Irwinton, Ga.), Dixie Tourist Court (Corinth, Miss.), Dixie Motor Lodge (Hattiesburg, Miss.), and Dixie Pines Motel (Bainbridge, Ga.). Some drew upon the region's history and legends, bringing us such lodging as the Robert E. Lee Motel (Gatlinburg), Robert E. Lee Motor Court (Richmond, Va.), Confederate Inn

(Biloxi), Rebel Inn (Memphis, Tenn.), and Brer Rabbit Motel (Dublin, Ga.). Doby's Hotel Court in Montgomery, Alabama, did not name itself after any specific person or event, but their logo, a cartoony Southern colonel with goatee and frock coat, was splashed across everything from their neon sign to items in the rooms themselves.

Most amusing of all are the motels whose names just did not seem to fit the area in which they were found, making them look like they had been picked up by a cyclone, like Dorothy's house, and plopped into the middle of a strange land. Tourism artist Warren Anderson once wrote of these displaced images that "their implicit message is that it is supposedly better to be somewhere else when you are already somewhere else." What better explanation could there be for the existence of the Coral Court in Rocky Mount, North Carolina; the Alabama Court in Panama City Beach, Florida; the Riviera Motel in Pigeon Forge; the Cherokee Tourist Camp in Chattanooga; the Mount Vernon Motel in Ocala, Florida; or the Anchor Motel in Birmingham, Alabama? Panama City Beach's Desert Palms Motel sounds more like it should be found in southern California, while the Miami Motel in Pearson, Georgia, defies all reasonable logic. The Western Air Motel in Fort Smith, Arkansas, went so far as to create a highly inappropriate neon saguaro cactus on its sign, while the Bamboo Motel in Saraland, Alabama, also seemed a bit out of its element. In some belief that people visiting Florida were in reality only using that state as an economical substitute for Hawaii, Fort Walton Beach brought us the Aloha Village, while St. Petersburg presented the Aloha Lodge.

One group of motels—or, more precisely, tourist courts—looked out of place on purpose. In 1933, entrepreneur Frank Redford opened a service station and restaurant on U.S. 31E at Horse Cave, Kentucky. There was nothing particularly unique about this, except that the building that housed both businesses was constructed to resemble a 60-foot-tall Indian tepee! It proved to be the roadside lure Redford was needing, and two years later he added to his business by constructing six smaller tepees as tourist cabins. He christened his enterprise the Wigwam Village.

In 1937, Redford built a second Wigwam Village in the same region, this time on U.S. 31W in Cave City, Kentucky. He announced that he planned to expand into a whole chain of Wigwam Villages, but the total number constructed finally reached only seven—five of which were in the Southern states. Over a period of ten years or so, Wigwam Villages opened in New Orleans (1940), Birmingham (1940), and Orlando (1948). (Outside the South, Villages ap-

peared in San Bernardino, California, in 1947 and Holbrook, Arizona, in 1950.) Records show that another location was planned for Luray, Virginia, in 1939, but never materialized.

It is obvious that, with the possible exception of the Arizona location, all of the Wigwam Villages looked whimsically displaced. They strove for an all-around Indian theme, from the uniforms worn by the employees to the souvenirs sold in their gift shops. Unfortunately, such eccentric motels fell victim to the increasing pressure from chains such as Holiday Inn, and the Wigwam Villages were so on headed for the Happy Hunting Grounds.

WIGWAM VILLAGE No. 5

UNITED MOTOR COURTS

Greetings from WIGWAM VILLAGE

Travel the WIGWAM WAY

4 Miles South of Birmingham, Ala. — On U.S. 11

BAMBOO MOTEL

There wasn't much bamboo in Saraland, Ala., but that didn't stop the Bamboo Motel from stalking tourists on U.S. 43.

Today, the only Southern location still standing is the one in Cave City, Kentucky, which is now benefitting from the public's reborn consciousness and appreciation for the golden era of highway travel.

Similar in concept to the wigwams (and just as misplaced) was the chain of Alamo Plaza Hotel Courts. Instead of an Indian motif, the Alamo Plazas were built as miniature replicas of the famous Spanish mission so important in Texas history. In fact, the Alamo Plaza locations in Texas and Oklahoma did not look particularly odd at all, but the same could not be said for them once they spread into the South. Shreveport and New Orleans (La.), Memphis (Tenn.), Jackson and Gulfport (Miss.), and Little Rock (Ark.) were not exactly the most appropriate spots for Spanish mission architecture . . . but when had that ever stopped the ever-innovative tourism industry?

The same regionality found in the South's motels extended to its roadside restaurants as well, although to a lesser extent. Obviously seafood was the bait that reeled tourists into seaside eateries such as the Happy Dolphin and the Sand Dollar in St. Petersburg, the Dunes in Gulf Shores, Alabama, and Captain Anderson's in Panama City Beach. In Cherokee, North Carolina, it was not surprising to find the Tee Pee Restaurant and the Sequoyah Restaurant. It would actually have been disappointing *not* to see the Black Bear Restaurant, Hungry Bear Restaurant, and Big Bear Restaurant in Gatlinburg, and the Smoky Mountain Pancake House in Pigeon Forge. For a brief time, another restaurant in Gatlinburg even licensed the Snuffy Smith comic strip hillbillies as its logo. The name of the Green Frog Restaurant in Waycross, Georgia, probably referred to that city's proximity to the Okefenokee Swamp, as well as the establishment's specialty, frog leg dinners. Even the "displaced" syndrome was alive and well on the Southern restaurant scene, with the Ole Smokey Restaurant found not in the mountains, but at Panama City Beach, the coastal-sounding Ship Ahoy Restaurant beached in Atlanta, and an Uncle Remus

Restaurant in Franklin, North Carolina . . . but the reason for its existence there is probably a long story worthy of the great tale-teller himself.

There were a number of eating spots in the South that today would be considered stereotypical, but at the time no one thought much about it. An extreme example would be Mammy's Shanty on Peachtree Street in Atlanta, which was still using somewhat surprising racial caricatures as late as 1968. (Its 24-hour companion next door was the Pickaninny Coffee Shop.) Also falling into this line, but with a little more class, would be Mammy's Cupboard in Natchez, Mississippi, which to this day continues to be housed in the crinoline skirt of a towering black lady.

Then there was the case of Aunt Fanny's Cabin in Smyrna, Georgia. More than an attempt to capitalize on Dixie history and make a fast buck, Aunt Fanny's was an enlarged actual slave cabin that had originally been built long before the Civil War. In fact, the living, breathing Aunt Fanny herself was on hand to greet visitors and welcome them into the home where she had once lived as a slave girl. Aunt Fanny finally went to her reward at the age of 104. And it should come as no surprise that the specialty of the house was . . . fried chicken.

Service stations, motels, restaurants—all of these were literal necessities for anyone making

ALAMO PLAZA HOTEL COURTS

Over 600 Rooms and Apartments In 9 Courts In 6 States

SHREVEPORT, LA.
MEMPHIS, TENN.

WACO, TYLER, AND BEAUMONT, TEXAS
OKLA. CITY, OKLA.
JACKSON, MISS.

LITTLE ROCK, ARK.
NEW ORLEANS, LA.

Like the Wigwam Villages, the Alamo Plaza motel chain used unusual architecture to catch the attention of passing motorists.

a trip of any length. But another type of business thrived along the Southern highways that could hardly have been considered essential, yet no vacation trip would have been complete without it. That was, of course, the souvenir shop.

Boxcars full of souvenirs were unloaded each year through the chain stores such as Stuckey's, Horne's, and Saxon's, but many more made their way into the small shops that sprang up wherever it looked like tourists might be congregating. The items they sold, long considered nothing

Seafood restaurants always reeled in beach visitors.

FAMOUS PLANTATION INN and MOTOR COURT — Six and One Half Miles South of SAVANNAH, GA.

Our Cottages are Immaculate. Best Beds, Tiled Stall Showers, Heated.

APPROVED AAA COURT

8A-H3164

ON HIGHWAY 17 — 6½ MILES SOUTH OF SAVANNAH

more than throwaway trash, have recently begun to be appreciated for what they are: relics of a lost era.

Florida's claim to fame in the souvenir biz was its seashell sculptures. Fashioned from stacks of actual shells gathered from the beaches, these almost surrealistic creations were often painted in fluorescent colors and festooned with plastic flamingos, palm trees, and leaping marlins. (Sometimes it seemed that Florida's souvenir industry would have gone defunct had it not been for these three omnipresent elements.) In the mountains, items made of

highly lacquered cedarwood were most common. Most of them simply had "Great Smoky Mountains" or some attraction's name stamped on them, rather than being modeled specifically for any one location.

Souvenirs of these types were available at practically any retail outlet in the Southern states. But there was one outlet that was truly unique in the amount of promotion it got…over a national radio network, no less. In the Ouachita Mountains of western Arkansas lay the remote community of Waters, where a fellow named Dick Huddleston ran a general store. Huddleston's store was no different from any of the other mercantiles that served the mountain communities, and Huddleston probably thought that his whole life would be spent in the obscurity of the backwoods countryside. But that was not to be.

Twenty-two miles west of Waters was the town of Mena, the hub of activity for that part of the state. Two young men in Mena grew to be friends of Huddleston through their frequent business trips to Waters. Their names were Chester Lauck and Norris Goff, and in 1931 they journeyed to Chicago and managed to land a spot on the NBC radio network, writing and performing a new comedy series known as *Lum and Abner*. Lauck was Lum and Goff was Abner, two elderly rural philosophers in a small town they called "Pine Ridge." More as an

dleston of the Lum and Abner program." He manufactured his own line of Lum and Abner souvenirs to sell, and for his crowning touch, in 1936 got the United States Post Office Department to change the name of Waters to Pine Ridge, to make it totally conform to the mythical radio storyline.

The demise of radio, taking *Lum and Abner* with it, removed Huddleston's once-thriving business, but he continued to keep the store open (more out of habit than anything else) until his death in 1963. The building was decrepit and about to fall apart when Ralph and Dorothy McClure, a couple from Fresno, California, discovered it on a visit to Arkansas in 1968. Realizing its historic value, they purchased the property from Huddleston's daughter and reopened it in January 1969 as a gift shop and museum. Today it is listed on the National Register of Historic Places and continues to attract old-time radio buffs from

inside joke than anything else, Lauck and Goff incorporated into Lum and Abner's conversations frequent mention of the "goin's on" over at "Dick Huddleston's store."

The power of radio in those Depression days should never be doubted. Soon Huddleston found his store swamped not with locals, but with tourists wanting to see the community being made famous by old Lum and Abner. Huddleston was only too happy to comply; he replaced the "J. R. Huddleston, General Merchandise" sign on the front of his building with an even larger one that read "Dick Hud-

Mammy's Shanty in Atlanta would today be considered extremely politically incorrect.

Dick Huddleston's store in Pine Ridge, Arkansas, was a typical general merchandise store until it was made famous by radio comedians Lum and Abner. It eventually became a museum and souvenir shop, which it remains today.

all over the country, including members of the National Lum and Abner Society.

So, now we have seen that roadside businesses in the South could take many forms, from giant international conglomerates like Kentucky Fried Chicken and Holiday Inn, to family-owned chains such as Stuckey's, to scores of small motels and restaurants, all the way down to a small-town general store that became a national landmark simply through its being mentioned on network radio. All of these places became somewhere for tourists to stop and spend some time on their way to their

eventual desinations. But if it is true that getting there was half the fun, what was the other half? Ah, but that is a question we shall begin unraveling in the *next* chapter. . . .

Peachy Beaches

Wherever the ocean comes into contact with the land, wonderful things are sure to happen.

—Anonymous

The philosopher who made the above observation is anonymous, but its truth is unquestionable. Sure, the South's mountain areas were beautiful and awe-inspiring, but after all, the North had mountains of its own. What the South did have, and the North did not, was the subtropical climate and white sandy beaches of the coastal areas. Therefore, it is not surprising that the beaches were the first regions to be developed specifically with tourist potential in mind.

As might be expected, not all of the Southern beach areas developed at the same time. Most of the region's earliest permanent settlements were on the coast, so such locales as Pensacola and St. Augustine were well known before such a thing as tourism was even thought of. The first glimmer of something special going on at the beach was when Henry Flagler, a tycoon in the infamous Standard Oil trust, honeymooned in St. Augustine in the winter of 1882. Since that was a particularly bad ice and snow season in

the North, the stark contrast warmed Flagler's heart and started ideas cooking in his head.

By 1885, he was making plans to build a luxury hotel in St. Augustine, an edifice he appropriately named the Ponce de Leon. However, he found that transportation facilities left much to be desired, and if he were going to attract his fabulously wealthy friends, great improvements needed to be made. Flagler accomplished this by first buying existing small railroad lines and tying them together, and then extending his own railroad further and further southward.

He had reached Daytona Beach by 1890, Palm Beach and West Palm Beach by 1894, and finally, Miami in 1896. (Within ten years, Flagler's railway would even be extended across the waters to the Florida Keys.) All of these resorts would become popular destinations for automobile travelers in later years, but they would always bear the mark of their beginning as playgrounds for the idle rich, who could now ride the rails all the way from New York City to Miami if they so desired. Ritzy hotels were built in all of them, and to this day, such adult diversions as gambling and nightclubbing still make

Hotel Ponce De Leon, St. Augustine, Florida

The Oldest City in the United States

up the bulk of southern Florida's appeal.

While Flagler was opening up the Atlantic coast of Florida, another railroad magnate, Henry Plant, was busy trying to attract travelers to the Gulf Coast side of the state, building similar luxurious accommodations at Tampa. While this city would also become a seaside resort, and scores of families would be attracted by the jungle atmosphere of Busch Gardens (see chapter 9), from the 1860s forward Tampa would be known primarily for the manufacture of cigars.

For all the early help given to Florida by the richer-than-rich, it was the arrival of the 1920s and the rise of automobile tourism that truly made the state a desirable destination for the general public. Much has been written about the famous Florida "land boom" of 1920–26, in which speculators made and lost fortunes by selling land (which happened to still be under water) to unsuspecting suckers...er, customers. Some permanent tourist sites were born out of this false prosperity, the major one being Miami Beach, a totally manmade spot created by automobile headlight manufacturer Carl Fisher (the father of the Dixie Highway, not coincidentally).

The advent of the automobile brought new attention to the already existing resorts on both Florida coasts, but the arrival of the middle class forced a change of pace for all of them. The whole idea behind catering to the very wealthy had been to give the "swells" a place where they could escape the hoi polloi, and now those very undesirables were invading

Wishing Well, Sausage Tree, Naranja, Fla. (20 miles so. of Miami) 388

This is a typical example of the sort of roadside attractions that sprang up along Florida's Atlantic coast. Here visitors could see the state's famous "sausage tree," toss coins into an "Aztec Wishing Well," and use the "Plighting Rock" to plight their troth!

Gatorland
ALLIGATOR FARM

World's Largest
Alligator Farm

2 MILES NORTH OF ST. AUGUSTINE
FLORIDA ON U. S. HIGHWAY NO. 1

the exclusive resorts with their rattling autos and uncouth ways. The millionaires were forced into jetting to Europe for their get-away-from-it-all jaunts, and the beaches were left to the general public. While a few of the old original luxury hotels managed to survive, many more were closed and boarded up as more economical means of accommodation—tourist courts and motels—sapped their business.

The attractions that could be found along Florida's Atlantic side had a distinctly different flavor from those along its Gulf side. Miami Beach always remained somewhat a wintering hole for the wealthy, so any families with children who happened to vacation there would just have to do the best they could to keep everyone entertained. For example, no attraction in the Miami area was promoted as heavily as the famous horse racing track at Hialeah, but this was hardly the sort of place for the kiddies—unless Junior had a few allowance bucks to bet on the nags.

Further north, it was automobile racing, not horses, that drew the biggest crowds. The fame of Daytona Beach, another of Flagler's early railroad stops, originated in the early years of the century,

The Daytona Beach strip during the 1960's.

when it was discovered that the sand on its beach was packed firmly enough to support the weight of the newfangled automobiles. The combination of the tropical atmosphere and the unique beach made Daytona a popular spot for automobile races. In 1903, speed demon Alexander Winton set a remarkable record of 68 miles per hour! Eventually, races on the beach gave way to today's famous Daytona 500, which continues to be the town's primary claim to fame.

This was also the region that gave birth to a tourism phenomenon whose influence would be felt across all of the seaside resorts. The idea was originally spawned by the success of the motion picture *Chang*. Producer Merriam Cooper (of *King Kong* fame) had developed a new way of obtaining footage of jungle animals by utilizing a "filming corral," which was large enough to contain the beasts while remaining imperceptible on film. A group of industrialists, some of whom happened to be associated with Cooper's studio, RKO Radio Pictures, came up with the notion that a similar facility could be used for filming *underwater* scenes. The spot they chose for their new movie studio was a desolate stretch of U.S. 1 just north of Daytona Beach and south of St. Augustine. However, it turned out that deciding on a location was the easiest part of the project. For one thing, marine biologists warned that there had been little or no prior success at keeping deep-sea creatures in captivity. Besides, an aquarium of adequate size to meet the needs of both the animals and the filmmakers had never before been attempted. And, finally—the point of most importance to our discussion here—the opinion was that "underwater movies" were not sufficiently in demand to financially support such a venture by themselves. The other problems would have to be worked out by a varied team of scientists, architects, and movie moguls, but there was a simple solution to this last one: Marine Studios, as the project was called, would be not only a movie studio but a *tourist attraction as well!* (And almost everyone today thinks it was Universal and the Disney/MGM Studios who came up with that idea.)

Marine Studios officially opened to visitors on June 23, 1938, making it one of Florida's oldest tourist attractions. In the 1940s, reflecting the facility's continuing emphasis on tourism rather than moviemaking, the name was changed from Marine Studios to Marineland; eventually, the name would be further altered to Marineland of Florida, after a sister attraction was opened in the Los Angeles area.

By the time of this 1955 postcard folder, Marineland's performing porpoises had become its biggest attraction.

Like all other attractions, Marineland ran into attendance problems with the United States' entry into World War II in 1941. The drop in tourist traffic was severe enough to cause the whole place to be completely shut down for the duration. Between 1942 and 1945, Marineland was handed over to the Coast Guard, which used its tanks for research and development of shark repellents and other worthwhile projects.

Marineland reopened in its civvies on

FABULOUS MIAMI SEAQUARIUM

March 1, 1946, just in time to greet the postwar baby boom. One innovation during this period would have far-reaching consequences in Florida's tourist industry. The facility's marine biologists had discovered that sea creatures such as porpoises were intelligent enough to be taught to perform. Not wasting any potential lure for more visitors, in 1951 Marineland debuted the world's first trained porpoise show! As any devoted Florida tourist can verify, performing porpoises would become an integral part of any beach resort. In fact, along with flamingos, palm trees, and marlins, they would eventually be a major icon of the Florida souvenir industry, but they were first introduced to the public

at Marineland.

Incidentally, what about the motion picture industry for which Marineland was first conceived? Well, even with all the tourists who were flopping around, Marineland/Marine Studios did manage to produce a number of motion pictures, although the vast majority of them fell into the documentary and short subject categories. One minor classic that emerged from the studio's depths in 1954 was that fish-faced freak *The Creature From The Black Lagoon.* Significantly, other movie studios began to take their cues from Marineland's way of doing things, but the only one that ever made much of a splash in Florida was the Ivan Tors Studio in Miami. Tors, famed for his performing animals, used his southern Florida studio to produce the famous TV series *Flipper,* which, in its own way, owed much to Marineland's pioneering performing porpoise projects. Other 1960s movies and TV shows to come out of the Tors Studio included *Daktari, Gentle Ben,* and *Clarence the Cross-Eyed Lion.*

With the success of Marineland, it was a foregone conclusion that imitators would eventually be swimming in from everywhere . . . if not for the moviemaking aspect of it, at least for the tourist potential. Because of this, for many years Marineland's methods of operation were kept TOP SECRET, and even protected by patents in some cases. However, during the mid-1950s the secrets began to leak out, and we all know how Marineland felt about any kind of leak. During 1955, two very similar attractions opened, ending Marineland's monopoly.

The Miami Seaquarium, opened on September 24, 1955, was an especially painful thorn in Marineland's blubber. Even today, Marineland's official history gets a little testy when it reports, "By the mid-1950s, the Miami Seaquarium had evidently gotten required information from former Marineland employees that enabled it to operate." Actually, some Florida historians report that Miami had an aquarium attraction several years before the advent of the Seaquarium. The story is that after a disastrous hurricane in the late 1920s—probably the same one that brought the land boom to a screeching halt—Miami's main thoroughfare, Biscayne Boulevard, found itself with a new feature: the hull of a giant ship, washed ashore by the storm, now sat projecting *over* the street! Some people recall that by the late 1940s this empty ship hull contained an aquarium of sorts, but today's Miami Seaquarium does not acknowledge this as part of their genesis. Whatever the "ship aquarium" was, it obviously made little or no mark on the rest of the industry.

A discussion of the other Marineland-inspired aquarium, the Gulfarium of Fort Walton Beach, will be coming up later in this chapter, but for now let's take a brief look at the other imitators that made soggy tracks across Florida. Down around the Keys, one could find the Theater of the Sea in Islamorada and Neptune's Garden in Marathon; the Aquatarium in St. Petersburg, the Sea-Orama in Clearwater Beach, and Ocean World in Fort Lauderdale proved that there was no end to the feeding frenzy initiated by Marineland. Eventually Sea World would flounder into Orlando, doing to aquarium attractions what Walt Disney World did to the rest of the industry.

Other than the aquariums, most of the amusement areas of Florida's Atlantic coast were patterned heavily after the boardwalk at Atlantic City, or perhaps even New York City's famed resort Coney Island. One amusement park, Pirates World, located in the small town of Dania, took this even more literally than the rest. While offering little that was very different from any other similar

Six years after its opening, the Miami Seaquarium made it onto the cover of the Standard Oil map of Florida.

Peachy Beaches

The Jacksonville Beach boardwalk in 1947.

endless array of amusement rides. It is said that at one time, Jacksonville Beach featured not one, not two, but *three* examples of each of the popular rides of the day: three Ferris wheels, three merry-go-rounds, three swing rides, and so forth. In nearby Atlantic Beach, when a storm caused a large house to topple onto the sand, some enterprising soul decided to turn it into the "Mystery House," one of those standard built-on-an-angle attractions that could be found in any good resort. (In chapter 4 we will see more examples of this genre that won fame in the Great Smoky Mountains.)

Besides the variance in their types of attractions, there was another factor that contributed to the different flavors of northern and southern Florida. The southern area remained a place where those who were financially able went during the winter to escape the deep freeze. From Daytona Beach northward, the beaches were summer resorts, where people from the rest of the South vacationed to get some ocean breezes on their backs during the heat of the season. It was almost a northern/southern hemisphere difference: the peak season in Jacksonville Beach was the off-season in Miami, and vice versa.

The beach that helped bridge the gap between the winter and summer seasons was Fort Lauderdale, which became renowned as the site of that annual youthful celebration of insanity

attraction, Pirates World did manage one feature that made it stand out from all the rest. This otherwise obscure playground became the final resting place for one of the rides that had been responsible for making Coney Island itself famous: the original 1897 Steeplechase ride, on which visitors rode brightly painted wooden horses over a roller-coaster-like track, played out its last days at Pirates World after its old home at Coney closed.

Jacksonville Beach featured its own Atlantic City-inspired boardwalk, lined with a seemingly

April to bask in Fort Lauderdale's giant cement pond proved irresistible. After the end of World War II, other college students got wind of what was going on, until every spring the Fort Lauderdale beaches were inundated with a writhing, sweating, party-till-you-drop mob of cabin fever-infected youth.

The Fort Lauderdale spring break and its accouterments became so nationally famous that it was even celebrated in popular music and motion pictures. Eventually the crowds grew to be too much for Fort Lauderdale to handle by itself, and the teenyboppers began spilling out into the other beach resorts. Today, high school and college students make a nightmare out of every Florida beach when spring arrives, but it all began in the place that was snubbed by Henry Flagler...who most likely could not rock and roll anyway.

Compared with the hullabaloo going on along the Atlantic Coast, the western side of Florida looked positively sedate. Heavy resort development centered around the vicinity of Tampa, Sarasota, St. Petersburg, and Fort Myers.

Regardless of what attractions took root in the area, St. Petersburg never fully managed to shake off the birthmark of its origin. While Flagler and his well-heeled comrades were

known as spring break. Unlike most of the other Atlantic Coast resorts, Fort Lauderdale was *not* one of Henry Flagler's creations; in fact, it was so insignificant that Flagler, convinced the place was worthless, instructed his staff to have his railroad bypass the community altogether.

Historians have traced the spring break tradition to the days when Fort Lauderdale decided to stand up for itself by building an Olympic-sized municipal swimming pool. To promote their new attraction, the city officials began issuing invitations to the rich kids at prominent northern Ivy League colleges to visit during their spring holidays and participate in highly publicized swimming competitions. The appeal of leaving the chilly colleges during March and pouring millions into Florida's Atlantic resorts, the Gulf side of the state was being settled by those less affluent souls who rattled South in their jalopies, camping along the side of the road as they went. These were the first tourists to make Tampa and St. Petersburg their resting spots, and many of them decided to retire and remain there permanently. This was the primary reason St. Petersburg came to be known first and foremost as an "old people's city."

Miami newspaper columnist Jack Kofoed reported of St. Petersburg in 1960: "Statistics indicate that 22% of the population is over 65 years of age, so much of the entertainment program is geared for those whose hair has grayed and muscles softened.... Ramps at every street crossing make it easier for shuffling feet, and 5,000 green benches enable the aging to rest their weary bones."

It was indeed St. Petersburg's famous green benches that became its trademark. The first bench, painted orange, was set out by a local real estate agent in 1908. Other businessmen followed suit by placing benches in front of their own stores, and it wasn't long before a city ordinance had to be passed to regulate the size of the benches and declare that they all be painted green. Second only to the green benches as a St. Petersburg symbol were its shuffleboard courts, especially appealing to its elderly population. It is not surprising, then, that one of St. Petersburg's eventual tourist attractions would be the Shuffleboard Hall of Fame.

Other attractions in the area very much followed the precedents set by other heavily-visited beach resorts. The Aquatarium filled the by-now-traditional porpoise show format of its predecessors, Marineland, the Miami Seaquarium, and the Gulfarium. The Florida Wild Animal and Reptile Ranch was present to satisfy all those whose trip to Florida would be incomplete without seeing a live alligator...or even a dead one, as this attraction contained a gift shop specializing in handbags made out of their own exhibits.

No tourist mecca would be complete without a sensational wax museum, so Josephine Tussaud's London Wax Museum arrived in St. Petersburg around 1963. (It took a sharp-eyed individual to catch the disclaimer that *Josephine* Tussaud's had no connection with the more famous *Madame* (Marie) Tussaud's museum in jolly olde England.) It boasted figures "so real you'll swear they are alive," depicting historical and hysterical personages, and featuring the all-too-common "chamber of horrors." In true roadside lure fashion, and to further cash in on the Tussaud name, the museum's signage was meant to resemble London's famous Big Ben tower.

Years before Universal Studios arrived in Orlando to go head-to-head with Disney's world, another movie studio had anchored itself to St. Petersburg. MGM's *Bounty* Exhibit (its full name) was touted as "Florida's only marine-historical attraction dedicated to the romance and history of an era long past." What was all the shouting about? Well, it seems that in 1960 MGM commissioned a full-scale working replica of the well-known sailing ship the *Bounty,* made famous by the movie about the mutiny on same. The replica was created for a big-budget remake of that classic 1935 film, which had starred Charles Laughton as Captain Bligh and Clark Gable as mutineer Fletcher Christian. The remake starred Marlon Brando, and while the original version is still revered among film history buffs, Brando's *Bounty* sank beneath the waves soon after its release in 1962. Trying to recoup their losses, MGM mothballed the *Bounty* adjacent to St. Petersburg's municipal pier and surrounded it with a bogus Tahitian village. Also included in the tour was

a reproduction of the longboat in which the real-life Captain Bligh and some of his sailors were set adrift following the famous mutiny in 1789. No one can say that MGM did not know

the difference between a hit and a miss, because tourists walking the decks of the *Bounty* exhibit heard scenes from the movie acted out by the voices of Laughton and Gable . . . *not* Brando, for whose version the replica was constructed!

Up at Tampa, the biggest attraction apart from the famous cigar factories was the African-themed Busch Gardens, which will be discussed in chapter 9. So will the vicinity's other "jungle" parks, including the Sarasota Jungle Gardens, St. Petersburg's Sunken Gardens, and the Tiki Gardens at Indian Rocks Beach. All made their

mark on the area's tourism history, but their influence on the beaches themselves was negligible. One of the more peculiar attractions to be found near Tampa was Treasureland, yet another seaside spot that capitalized on the "pirate" theme so popular at such resorts. The odd thing about Treasureland, though, was that it was an indoor "dark ride" of the type made famous by the Disney and Six Flags parks.

Would-be privateers were taken in miniature galleons "through an exciting and rib-tickling adventure in piracy brought to life by electronic animation . . . through the refuge of the swamp and a riproaring battle at sea. You'll laugh as the mutinous crew celebrates their victory, and then witness the destructive power of a hurricane which reclaims the gold and jewels. Under the sea, you'll watch the creatures of the deep hold their own celebration." If this sounds vaguely like a cover version of Disney's Pirates of the Caribbean ride, you are probably right. However, at the time of Treasureland's operation, Pirates of the Caribbean existed only at Disneyland in California. Obviously the arrival of the real thing at Walt Disney World made Tampa's Treasureland walk the plank. It should be noted, though, that while it existed Treasureland was probably the only case of a dark ride standing as an attraction all its own, rather than being part of another amusement park.

Then there was Sarasota, where one giant theme prevailed over any other: the circus! In today's world of indoor coliseums and such, the circus is just as likely to come to town in January and February as at any other time, but there are many who can still remember the olden days when the arrival of the big tents and wild animals was a sure sign of spring or summer. In that era, circuses usually spent the off season in some warm climate . . . and it so happened that the Ringling Brothers and Barnum and Bailey Circus wintered in Sarasota . . . so it was inevi-

table that in that area the big top would be the big draw.

John Ringling used the money his circus had taken in to build a mansion of epic proportions in Sarasota during the 1920s, and he filled it with priceless art objects from around the world. Ringling supposedly developed his interest in fine art while traveling around Europe, scouting out new acts for his circus. There are those who have raised an eyebrow or two at the odd juxtaposition of high-culture art and the lowbrow appeal of the circus, but John Ringling proved that selling tickets, popcorn, and peanuts could indeed make one a wealthy man. His legacy lives on in two distinctly different forms in the area: the Ringling Art Museum presents the impresario's collection of paintings and sculpture, with nary a clown or seltzer bottle in sight, while the other side of the ring is relegated to the Circus Hall of Fame.

Further down the coast, near Ft. Myers, a

Cape Coral Gardens in Fort Meyers was one of the most spectacular failures in Southern tourism history.

park opened in the mid-1960s that seemed to try to cram a half dozen Florida stereotypes into one attraction. Known as Cape Coral Gardens, this mishmash appeared to be modeled somewhat after Cypress Gardens at Winter Haven, but with a touch of the Marineland porpoise show thrown in, somehow intertwined with a sailing ship that resembled the *Bounty* and art exhibits that attempted to out-ringle Ringling.

Even its advertising sounded like the place was positively beside itself: "Cape Coral Gardens has something for every member of the family, from thrilling action events to quiet, serene beauty, from memorable classical music to magnificent sculpture, from dramatic fountains to sleepy lagoons." This was obviously a case of trying to be all things to all people, and the attraction soon found itself crushed, maimed, and mangled by its own weight. It did not even survive to be killed by the theme park era; on Labor Day 1970, the gates were locked and the entire complex left to deteriorate into ruin. Today, Cape Coral Gardens is hardly more than a fuzzy memory, almost like a bad dream.

We have seen how the development along Florida's east and west coasts came about gradually over a period from the 1880s onward. However, there was another coastline that was almost totally ignored until well after the Great Depression, only to become one of the most famous of all. We are speaking, of course, of the famed "Miracle Strip" of the state's northern Gulf beaches, anchored by those powerhouse resorts Panama City Beach and Fort Walton Beach.

The Florida Panhandle, as the geographic region is known, was long considered barely a part of the state at all. With Pensacola its only notable city, the Panhandle and its beaches had not seen anything near the type of frantic tourist activity pioneered by the millionaires on the Atlantic coast. There is a very good reason why the tourism potential of the Panhandle beaches remained undeveloped for so long. They lacked one very important element that was required to attract large crowds of automobile tourists. That one element was a road.

There was only one way to reach the sugar-white sands of Panama City Beach and Fort Walton Beach, and it was not by land. In 1908, the *Panama City Pilot* newspaper reported on its front page: "It is already very evident that about everyone who visits this bay desires to go to the gulf beach and take a dip in the surf. There is scarcely a night but there are from one to five boat loads of people going there even now... it has been suggested that a small landing dock should be built, which would greatly facilitate the landing of parties on the gulf beach." The story was similar in Fort Walton, which had originally been established as *Camp* Walton during the Civil War (the name was not changed officially until 1931). Would-be tourists left Pensacola by boat and sailed down the coast to the slowly-developing community.

Even the construction of U.S. 98 during the early 1930s did not totally solve the problem. The original route of the highway did not take it to the water's edge, so even those who arrived by automobile were faced with either a long walk to the beach, or, in some cases, physically pushing their cars through the sand. In 1935, businessman Gid Thomas decided to confront this drawback by hauling in seashells from

Appalachicola, and using them to pave a road leading to the beaches. Whereas most resorts developed slowly and almost imperceptibly over a long period of time, it is a matter of historic record that Panama City Beach was formally opened to the public on May 2, 1936.

Tourist cabins and cottages were built along the newly-accessible beaches, but true roadside attractions had to wait until the postwar tourism boom. By 1954, the main feature at Panama City Beach was Long Beach Resort, a Coney Island-like conglomeration that emulated the older boardwalk flavor of Jacksonville Beach and its Atlantic Coast contemporaries. A small amusement park and the bathing beach itself were the main features, along with "the Hangout," a combination snack bar and dance floor that proved to be a favorite of wild, uninhibited youth. During the 1960s, most of Long Beach Resort's tourists moved across U.S. 98 to the Western-themed Petticoat Junction amusement park

Long Beach Resort, Panama City Beach's first major tourist draw, as seen in the late 1940s.

DON'T MISS SEEING

Florida's

Gulfarium

Living Sea

UNDERWATER PORPOISE FEEDING

US 98

...In the Heart of the "MIRACLE STRIP" —at— FORT WALTON BEACH, FLA.

GULFARIUM

(discussed in chapter 9). Today, little physical evidence of the old resort remains, save for a few preserved cottages. The Hangout became more like a wipeout when Hurricane Eloise got it in her clutches in 1975, but in the summer of 1996 it was rebuilt...although in a more upscale part of the beachscape rather than at its original location.

Another attraction originating during this early period was the Snake-A-Torium, one of probably a half million reptile farms that dotted the South's tourist highways. While most others came and went, the Snake-A-Torium established itself as a major (if somewhat creepy) presence in Panama City Beach's lineup, and held that spot for some four decades. In best roadside attraction fashion, its billboards began near the Alabama state line and appeared every few miles until visitors were led by the forked tongue into the parking lot. Finally succumbing to a fall from grace of the traditional reptile farm, the Snake-A-Torium shed its skin and was renamed "Zooworld"

during the 1990s. It has tried valiantly to live down its former image ever since. Veteran beach visitors remember, however.

One sure sign that Panama City Beach was on its way was the opening of a local Stuckey's store in August 1954. Its owners, Dennis and Martha Rich, recalled that at that time it was highly unusual to see one car pass their shop every fifteen minutes. Its closest neighbor was the Snake-A-Torium, whose owner used to trap water moccasins in the marshy area that surrounded the candy store.

By this time, the entire area stretching from Pensacola to Panama City had been dubbed the "Miracle Strip," a term coined in 1952. Sitting in the middle of this stretch, Fort Walton Beach soon found that it was going to need some attractions of its own if it were going to carve out its own niche in the tourism industry. It has been pointed out that the community's name is full of discrepancies, as it was never the site of a fort and there are no beaches within its city limits! For that, tourists had to travel over a swing-style bridge to Okaloosa Island. Prior to 1950, Fort Walton Beach was known more for its (illegal) gambling industry—hardly the sort of thing that would attract a lot of families to the area.

The answer to Fort Walton's need for attention came in August 1955, when the Gulfarium opened as the *second* such marine-themed

By the late 1960s, Panama City Beach's strip was lined with attractions that were colorful, exotic, and goofy.

attraction in the state (following Marineland, of course, but predating the Miami Seaquarium by a scant month). Like the others, it was first conceived for serious marine biological research, but its tourist attraction status was necessary to pay the bills. The main factor that distinguished it from the other two was that it concentrated solely upon the denizens of the Gulf of Mexico, rather than the Atlantic Ocean. Marine researcher Brandy Siebenaler found the then-isolated location on Okaloosa Island, and began construction on the facility

in September 1954. Eleven months later, the Gulfarium opened to splashing success, in a bright aqua-and-yellow facility that sported a large cutout porpoise as its main decoration on the front, an emblem that identified the attraction for years. In 1995, Hurricane Opal nearly washed the Gulfarium out to sea, but the aquarium was able to rebound from that setback. However, due to this natural disaster and creeping modernization, the Gulfarium bears little physical resemblance to its 1955 appearance.

An aerial view of Panama City Beach's monster Miracle Strip Amusement Park.

Even with all of these developments, the phenomenal growth of the Miracle Strip did not really shift into full gear until circa 1960. By that time, the three anchor resorts (Panama City Beach, Fort Walton Beach, and Pensacola Beach) had become homes for those museums of elaborate concrete sculpture, the Goofy Golf courses (discussed in chapter 5). Shortly thereafter, Panama City Beach surged ahead of all the others—and, for that matter, the older established Florida beach resorts—by opening its famed Miracle Strip Amusement Park.

More than anything else, the 1962 appearance of this park was the push that propelled Panama City Beach into its present-day prominence. Nothing about it was small; smothered in multicolored electric lights and boasting what was claimed to be the fastest roller coaster in America, Miracle Strip Amusement Park made all earlier comparable efforts look like cheap traveling carnivals. For some reason, it was especially obsessed with haunted house attractions, prominently featuring no fewer than three of the supernatural abodes. One, the

Hurricane House, had a rather ironic name, considering the repeated buffets the resort would take from real-life storms later in its life. The aptly-named Old House (not to be confused with the historic Oldest House in St. Augustine) attracted visitors with a spectral figure that walked around on its roof. The third ghostly grotto took the form of a medieval castle, with a surrealistically disturbing façade depicting a huge dragon leering at a broken clock that was striking 13, accompanied by recorded, cartoony "sproing" sound effects (go figure *that* one out).

The other U.S. 98 resorts knew when they were licked, and none of them even attempted to compete with Panama City Beach's monolith park. Fort Walton was content with its tiny Okaloosa Island Park, while Pensacola Beach just never quite got into the whole amusement park rat race. The quiet fishing community of Destin, situated just east of Fort Walton, shunned *all* tacky tourist development for many years; until the 1990s, its only bow to the passing motorists was its huge green concrete knight, the emblem of the Green Knight Restaurant (later a lounge and liquor store).

The Green Knight was only one example of the giant concrete figures that called the Miracle Strip their home. Angelo's Steak Pit in Panama City Beach used a blockbuster bull to steer tourists into its parking lot. Another restaurant, the

Sir Loin Steakhouse, constructed a giant knight (not green) who was advertised as the "largest known statue in Florida" (it always *looked* like there was a competition going on in this realm, but this claim proved that it was indeed a reality!). When the steakhouse went out of business and was converted into the Shell Island Gift Shop, Sir Loin himself also got plastic surgery and a paint job, emerging as King Neptune. The frozen soft drink Icee really established a beachhead in Panama City, with a row of gigantic Icee drink cups serving as roadside refreshment stands during the 1960s. Next door to the accurately named Goofy Golf course, a concrete replica of Icee's trademark, a thirsty polar bear, enticed hot vacationers into another snack bar. The Icee cups eventually melted into history, only to be replaced by some even larger ice cream cones, which in turn were devoured by encroaching modernization along the strip.

Certain elements can be found in any major tourist area: amusement parks, wax museums,

The Icee Bear and friends quench their thirst.

The Panama City Beach observation Tower.

haunted houses, wacky miniature golf courses, reptile farms, and the like. One more item that should be added to that list is the omnipresent observation tower, offering little but an elevator ride that ends in a panoramic view of the surrounding area. (Ideally, the surrounding area should in turn offer something to be seen, but, as illustrated by such cases as the Citrus Tower in Clermont, Florida, which sits in the middle of nothing but orange groves, this is not always necessary.) Panama City Beach rose high above its competition with the opening of its own 200-foot observation tower in 1965. The gleaming white edifice was so futuristic in design, it looked like it might have been created by George Jetson. For thirty years, adults, teen-agers, and children ascended the tower for an unparalleled view of the garish Miracle Strip, until Hurricane Opal spelled its

demise. It was demolished in December 1995 to make way for a six-story condominium.

In one aspect of Florida tourism, Panama City Beach came to find itself a follower rather than a leader. As the 1970s arrived, so did the somewhat shocking realization that PCB had absolutely no aquarium attraction to go head-to-hammerhead with the Gulfarium and its ilk. Consequently, 1970 saw the arrival of Gulf World, a somewhat smaller version of the larger aquariums. Concentrating more on showmanship than on marine biology, Gulf World looked right at home along the gaudy strip...although to this day it has never become quite as famous as its ancestors.

The attractions of the Miracle Strip eventually came to almost totally replace the older resorts on the Atlantic coast, probably because they were geographically closer to the rest of the country. (As we have seen, Miami Beach was, and always will be, of a different slant.) In the 1980s and 1990s, though, some people began taking a second look at what this tourist-happy stretch of U.S. 98 had become. In 1994, critic Tom Fiedler wrote that "the Panama City Beach strip could serve as a model of how not to develop a natural resource . . . the gorgeous beach has been mugged and gagged, left nearly invisible from the highway." Even the name "Miracle Strip" seemed overtly to remind people of the area's kooky reputation, so today most of the Chambers of Commerce have adopted the more serene moniker "the Emerald Coast." The giant ice cream cones have disappeared, and the few remaining old 1950s-style miniature golf courses now face competition from beautifully landscaped courses that attempt to blend in with the environment. It is truly a change, but which version of tourism do the tourists themselves prefer? Well, since the Miracle Strip—ahem, Emerald Coast—resorts are now attracting just as many visitors as they did in the old days (if not more), apparently that question is quite beside the point.

Mention the word "beaches," and the first thing that comes to most people's minds is "Florida." But while Florida seemed to have a monopoly on the South's seaside, there were still other states that set out to develop their own coastlines for maximum tourist appeal. With a few exceptions, most of them ended up as "spillover" spots from Florida, but they deserve a look anyway.

The coastal area west of Pensacola Beach earned its own nickname, but one less flattering than that of the Miracle Strip. From Gulf Shores, Alabama, over to Biloxi, Mississippi, the beaches were unofficially known as the "Redneck Riviera." The commercial development along these beaches tended to live up to this designation, generally imitating the Miracle Strip in a low-budget sort of way. Gulf Shores, for example, was characterized by the Flora-Bama, a sleazy sort of bar whose claim to fame was that the building straddled the two state lines. There was a small amusement park and a couple of dinosaur-laden miniature golf courses, but they paled in comparison to any of their Florida contemporaries. A landmark of the Gulf Shores strip was the Lighthouse Motel, whose main office was built to resemble just that.

Gulf Shores' appearance—indeed, its very demeanor—was altered forever when Hurricane Frederic came roaring ashore in 1979. Overnight, most of the area's older structures were obliterated, and the community was forced to begin building anew. Tired of its "Redneck Riviera" reputation, businesspeople in Gulf Shores set to work to improve their lot, and today the area is one of the South's most modern beach resorts. Condominiums and highly landscaped miniature golf courses have totally replaced the dinky little motels and folk-art courses of the 1950s and 1960s. Even the Lighthouse Motel has switched over to a more resort-oriented approach . . . all the while maintaining its lighthouse-shaped roadside lure, for tradition's sake.

Other than Gulf Shores, Alabama's only other contribution to the Gulf Coast was Dauphin Island, a barrier just south of Mobile.

Development of the island was hindered somewhat by the fact that until 1955 there was no way to reach it except by boat. In that year, a bridge was built and electricity arrived for the first time, but except for some slight motel development Dauphin Island never became much of a total vacation destination. It remains today known mainly for its bird sanctuary.

Mississippi's slight brush with the Gulf of Mexico followed much the same pattern as Gulf Shores. The hub of activity here was Biloxi, with its own ramshackle version of an amusement park. Running a close second was Gulfport. By this time, it looked like aquarium attractions in Florida had fished for every variation on a catchy name, so when Gulfport hauled in its own entry in the seaweed stakes, it had to be content with calling it, rather unimaginatively, Marine Life. An honest-to-goodness lighthouse, not an ersatz one like the roadside lighthouses found in the tourist industry, beamed some much-needed distinction to the Biloxi/Gulfport area as well.

At least history was on the Mississippi Gulf Coast's side, as it was the location for Beauvoir, the residence of dethroned Confederate president Jefferson Davis. After Davis's death in 1889, his house was used as a sort of nursing home for former Confederate soldiers and sailors, but when the last of them had whistled "Dixie" for the final time, Beauvoir was restored and opened to tourists in 1941.

Like Gulf Shores, the Biloxi region found salvation from its "Redneck Riviera" period through a natural disaster. Ten years before Hurricane Frederic, in 1969, the even more vengeful Hurricane Camille slammed the everlasting daylights out of Biloxi, and what was rebuilt was done with so much care that any resemblance to its former self was strictly unintentional. The big deal

for Biloxi came when gambling was legalized, paving the way for the endless string of casinos and nightclubs that give the Mississippi Gulf Coast its present-day fame. Perhaps these developments, for good or bad, have finally given the area an identity of its own . . . not just as a poor man's Panama City.

On the South's other coast, development north of Jacksonville Beach, Florida, fell into two main categories: playgrounds for the rich and Atlantic City wannabes. The best example of the first category would have to be Jekyll Island, Georgia. In 1886, shortly after Henry Flagler began his escapades in Florida, a group of wealthy families purchased Jekyll Island and made a private resort out of it. (One would-be comedian wisecracked that Jekyll Island is where the wealthy went to hyde. Oh, dear.) Such loaded luminaries as the Rockefellers, Morgans, and Vanderbilts held court until 1947, when the state of Georgia purchased the island from the highly exclusive Jekyll Island Club and set about preparing it for the common tourist. Today, true to its name, Jekyll Island has something of a split personality. On one side of the island is the historic district, with the preserved structures of the elite, while the other side of the island is devoted to families and their kids, with motels, miniature golf, and all the rest.

The best example of the Coney Island/ Atlantic City style outside Florida was Myrtle Beach, South Carolina. It even featured its own version of the Miracle Strip, here dubbed the Grand Strand. Incredible miniature golf courses became one of Myrtle Beach's trademarks, and the resort boasted an amusement park, the Myrtle Beach Pavilion, that would have been in direct competition with Panama City Beach's park, had the two been located anywhere near each other. Myrtle Beach also contained Pirateland, a tacky kiddie spot in the best beach tradition.

North of Myrtle Beach stretched a series of other sandy pleasure spots, but while they all had their own loyal followings, the fact that hardly anyone thinks of the beach when considering North Carolina or Virginia proves that, regardless of how passionate their regular visitors felt about them, they were doomed to be forever considered also-rans in the beach tourist race. (Fittingly, the two states' mountain attractions far overshadowed any activity going on along their shores.) Obviously, the further north one went, the less tropical the climate became,

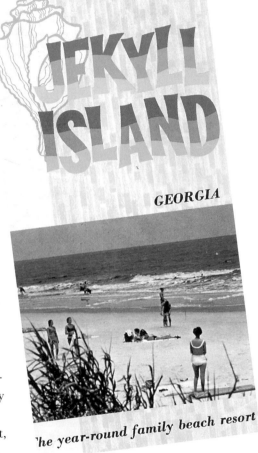

JEKYLL ISLAND

GEORGIA

the year-round family beach resort

mer meant spending "a few weeks at the seashore"; as times changed, vacations became shorter and shorter, until now very few people spend more than one weekend in any given spot. Compounding already existing problems, the concentration of theme parks in central Florida had the effect of siphoning tourists away from the state's long-established beach areas. Even that longtime bailiwick for buddies of the briny blue, Marineland, was forced to file for bankruptcy in the spring of 1998.

A final, and less obvious, contributor toward the decline of the beaches' monopoly on tourism was the development in the 1930s of an alternate region in which to spend some valuable vacation time. As we are about to see, those who were tired of the beach could now set their sights a bit higher, and strike out for the mountains!

and this factor, aside from Florida's sheer drawing power, probably played a big part in the secondary nature of these beaches.

So, in looking back over the past century, what has been the major change in the way people look at the South's beaches? Well, the disappearance of the exclusive luxury resorts, such as Jekyll Island and Henry Flagler's endless stream of Florida communities, was the first big switch. When automobile tourists, and later whole families, became the targeted customers, the beach industry entered its second phase. Even that was relatively short-lived, however, because of the changing nature of family vacations themselves. Old-timers in the resort business remember fondly the days when sum-

Head fer the Hills

In the Blue Ridge Mountains of Virginia,
On the trail of the lonesome pine. . . .

—Famous song, origin unknown

For decades, the Southern mountains were considered somewhat second rate, at least as far as being used as a vacation destination. Geologically speaking, they had been present for at least as long as the beaches, possibly even longer, yet it took considerably more time for the tourist industry to realize their commercial potential.

A large factor in this was the simple matter of accessibility. While railroads, and then highways, were laid down to create tourist routes to the beaches, the mountains of the South proved to be just as difficult to navigate as they had been for Davy Crockett and his pioneer peers who hacked their way through their underbrush. However, in the latter half of the nineteenth century and the early years of the twentieth, the "primitive" culture of the isolated mountain communities began to attract serious scholars of folklore. The resulting publication of their studies brought, for the first time, information to the general public as to just what was going on back in those hills.

There were such books as *In The Tennessee Mountains* (1884), *The Prophet of the Great Smoky Mountains* (1885), *Down in Arkansas* (1902), *On A Slow Train Through Arkansaw* (1903), *Trail of the Lonesome Pine* (1908), *Three Years In Arkansaw* (1908), *Our Southern Highlands* (1922), *Mountain Homespun* (1931), and *Ozark Mountain Folk* (1932). Some of these were works of fiction, some were serious documentation, and some were little more than joke books at the hill country's expense. At the same time, organizations such as the Tennessee Valley Authority were helping to bring mountain life to the public's attention, frequently portraying the inhabitants of the Southern highlands as impoverished, ignorant, and no better off than denizens of undeveloped Third World countries.

In the 1920s and 1930s, the stereotypical "hillbilly" image really bloomed in all forms of media. The comic strip adventures of Li'l Abner (originally set in Kentucky) and Snuffy Smith (specified as North Carolina) both began in 1934. Motion pictures of the period also jumped on the hayseed hay wagon, with such titles as *Them Thar Hills, Silly Billies,* and *Mountain Music.* On the radio, the lovable *Lum and Abner* (whom we met back in chapter 2) spun their yarns of life in Pine Ridge, Arkansas, although to their credit they discarded the typical barefoot hillbilly image for a more realistic portrayal of a small Southern mountain community.

Radio's most influential contribution toward attracting attention to the Southern hills was its quick adoption of country music. By the mid-1920s, radio stations in most major markets began featuring regular "barn dance" shows, which brought local talent in to fiddle, whistle, stomp, and generally have a cotton-pickin' good time. The entry in this dulcimer derby that had the most effect on the South was first broadcast from WSM in Nashville in 1925, with the unoriginal title *The WSM Barn Dance.*

The WSM Barn Dance featured a regular procession of mountain fiddlers, singers, and other nonprofessionals, emceed by a former Memphis newspaper writer named George D. Hay who took on the stage name of "the Solemn Ole Judge." It was in 1927 that one of Hay's ad-libs changed the name of the show (and Southern music) forever. *The WSM Barn Dance* inexplicably followed a network broadcast of classical music, and after one of those shows, Hay made the remark that "For the past hour we have been listening to selections taken largely from grand opera, but now we're goin' to get down to earth with some *Grand Ole Opry!*"

The title of *The WSM Barn Dance* did not change overnight, but after Hay's remark more and more listener mail started referring to the Saturday night shindig as *The Grand Ole Opry,* and the Opry it became. Soon interested listeners, mainly from the farmlands surrounding Nashville, began showing up on the radio studio's doorstep, hoping for a glimpse at the goings on inside. Several of them even brought their own instruments along, in hopes of being put on the air. (Sometimes they actually were!) WSM being a clear channel station, people all over America were able to tune in on *The Grand Ole Opry,* and soon it had become a broadcasting phenomenon.

Tourists who made their way to Nashville were often there specifically to watch the weekly *Opry* broadcast. This initially did not sit too well with Nashville's aristocratic city fathers. For years, they had promoted Nashville's image as "the Athens of the South," a seat of learning

hill country folk who played the old-time tunes that had been handed down for generations. These folk songs also helped popularize the idyllic and/or nostalgic image of the mountain regions. The various string bands that played on the show were given evocative names like the Possum Hunters, the Gully Jumpers, the Fruit Jar Drinkers, and so on. When the legendary Roy Acuff joined the show in 1938, his group was called the Crazy Tennesseans, but fearing that the name might be perceived by some as derogatory, they soon became the more inspiring Smoky Mountain Boys.

The number of out-of-town visitors and tourists who flocked to it each week required that the broadcast be moved from site to site around Nashville as it outgrew each location. The locale that most immediately comes to the mind of anyone familiar with the Opry in those days is the Ryman Auditorium. Originally built in the 1890s as a tabernacle for religious services, the Ryman became the home of *The Grand Ole Opry* in 1943. For the next thirty years, hundreds of thousands of tourists waited patiently in line to enter the imposing brick structure to hear Acuff sing "Wabash Cannonball," see Grandpa Jones whale the cookies out of his banjo, or listen to Minnie Pearl tell stories about the fictitious happenings down in Grinder's Switch.

The influx of paying tourists, and the rise of

and culture. In 1897, they even went so far as to construct their own replica of the Greek Parthenon, to lend credence to their claim. But now what were they becoming known for throughout the country? That "hillbilly music" program, that's what! The Nashville elite were horrified.

And "hillbilly music" was a good term for what audiences heard on the original *Grand Ole Opry*. Unlike today's high-priced, high-power talent that makes up the show, early Opry performers were by and large Southern big-money recording studios, eventually caused Nashville to change its mind about *The Grand Ole Opry*. They decided that since it was useless to fight against the "hillbillies," they might as well join the clan, and the "Athens of the South" finally became "Music City USA." Practically everything promoting the city now revolved around country music and its stars, from tourist brochures to restaurants to motels.

By the dawn of the modern tourism era in 1971, the Ryman Auditorium's neighborhood had undergone a prodigious change. Hoping to lure away some of the multitudes that gathered to see the Opry, the streets around the old building became a nightmarish jungle of seedy nightclubs, bars, massage parlors, and other such enterprises definitely *not* aimed at the family trade. The Opry's promoters were concerned about maintaining the show's image, so in 1972 they built a large Walt Disney World-like theme park, Opryland USA, and announced that in a short time the weekly radio broadcast would move out of the Ryman and into a brand-new, specially-built Opry House in the park.

This news was greeted with the same mixed emotions as when the new interstate program had replaced the old federal highways. There was much sadness over the loss of tradition that the Ryman Auditorium represented, but deep down, everyone knew that the outdated, aging edifice was really no longer suited to the

An early hotel in the mountain resort of Hot Springs, Arkansas.

type of broadcast the Opry had become. So, on March 10, 1974, *The Grand Ole Opry* made its debut from its new home in Opryland, and the Ryman was put in mothballs. Fortunately, in recent years the old auditorium has been restored and is now being used again for musical performances by country music stars. The Opryland theme park laid down its fiddle and quit at the end of its 1997 operating season, but *The Grand Ole Opry* lives on, twanging away from the 1974 Opry House.

When the early Opry performers left their mountain homes to make the journey to Nashville, little did they realize that their old, remote neighborhoods would eventually become just as popular with tourists as the big cities. There

Observation Tower, Hot Springs, Arkansas

is one factor that makes the tourism development of the mountains different from any other facet of the industry: while most tourist areas were the work of individuals, the mountains of the South might never have seen any attractions at all had it not been for the United States Government.

The National Park System was responsible for bringing people to these formerly unexplored regions. It all had its beginnings back in 1832, when President Andrew Jackson designated the area around Hot Springs, Arkansas, as a Federal Reservation, the idea of national parks not yet having been created. The thermal waters of Hot Springs proved to be the biggest attraction of all, particularly in the early days. Elaborate turn-of-the-century bath houses and hotels can still be found in the city today, Hot Springs not being as obsessed with modernization as some other tourist towns.

Of course, one can spend only so much

time bathing, so Hot Springs soon developed other ways to separate tourists from their money. 1902 saw the beginning of the Arkansas Alligator Farm, which set out to prove that those toothy, scaly swamp denizens were not an exclusive feature of Florida. H. L. Campbell imported the ragged-toothed reptiles from the southern portion of Arkansas because of, as the company's official history put it, "the need for some type of tourist attraction due to the great influx of people who at that time came to take the Hot Thermal Baths, and there were no attractions other than the natural resources." Good enough reason in the tourism biz!

The Josephine Tussaud Wax Museum, which we visited back in St. Petersburg, also set up shop in Hot Springs, with subjects ranging from Alfred Hitchcock to the Last Supper. For those antsy kids, leery of any vacation destination whose primary business was taking a bath, there was the I.Q. Zoo, with animal performers whose I.Q.'s just may have outranked those of many of their visitors. There was also Tiny Town, an animated miniature city whose inhabitants were only three inches tall, giving children a temporary Gulliver complex.

As we saw in chapter 3, it would seem that observation towers are a necessary feature of any tourist spot, but Hot Springs raised theirs first. There was a 75-foot tower on top of Hot Springs Mountain as far back as 1877, built by

image of the bewhiskered, moonshiner variety of hillbilly more firmly established, and much to the dismay of those who wanted a more positive reputation for the state, this caricature remains the emblem of the Ozarks today.

Unlike other regions, for many years the Ozarks never really developed one all-powerful tourist city in its midst, such as Gatlinburg in the Great Smoky Mountains, Miami Beach on the Atlantic Coast, or Panama City Beach on the Gulf coast. That designation would eventually fall to Branson, Missouri, but not until the 1980s. Up to then, probably the most visited single town in the Ozarks was Eureka Springs, originally famed for its therapeutic mineral waters but later known mainly for its religious emphasis. This aspect of the town did not originate until 1965, with the organization of the Elna M. Smith Foundation, whose purpose was to preserve religious artifacts for future generations. (In this regard, it seems to have been patterned after a much older and more obscure attraction, Fields of the Wood, near Murphy, North Carolina.) The Foundation's best-known creation was the Great Passion Play, one of several outdoor dramas in the South, but perhaps the only one that did not deal with local history. A giant Christ statue

one Enoch Woolman. When that wooden structure was wiped out by lightning and fire, a second, 165-foot tower (made of steel this time) replaced it. It must be admitted that this version's original appearance more closely resembled a forest ranger's fire tower than a tourist draw. The austere observation point survived for more than sixty years despite its esthetics, and today's 216-foot Hot Springs Mountain Tower, completed in 1983, presents a more enticing and up-to-date appearance.

In the northern part of Arkansas, the Ozark Mountains did not have the same kind of benefits that resulted from National Park status elsewhere in the South's hill country, but they more than made up for that with their place in legend and folklore. Nowhere else was the

VIRGINIA-NORTH CAROLINA
BLUE RIDGE
Parkway

ADDRESS INQUIRIES TO
NATIONAL PARK CONCESSIO
Blue Ridge Parkway Operati
LAUREL SPRINGS, NORTH CAROLINA

In 1949, the city of Roanoke erected this giant neon star atop Mill Mountain. It has been a landmark ever since.

and the New Holy Land (similar to the Ave Maria Grotto we will visit in chapter 6) also made Eureka Springs a popular religious pilgrimage.

Other Ozark attractions were scattered far and wide, rather than concentrated in any one particular area. Mountain Village 1890 was established near Bull Shoals, Arkansas, in 1961. While at first glance it might have given the appearance of a typical artificial recreation of a hill country community, closer inspection proved that the buildings that made up Mountain Village 1890 were actually moved in from real-life nineteenth-century towns throughout the northern Arkansas hills, so their authenticity could never be questioned in the least. Unfortunately, the same cannot be said for Booger Holler, a "manufactured" attraction in the most tacky hillbilly vein, whose advertising slogan has been given for years as "Population 9, Countin' One

Hound Dawg." Booger Holler has never looked like anything more than a poor man's imitation of Dogpatch USA, the *Li'l Abner* theme park discussed in chapter 5.

After President Theodore Roosevelt began the National Park program in the early 1900s, it took a little while for the government to get around to setting aside any land in the Appalachian Mountains, but when they did, *two* National Parks were created that, though over 400 miles apart, would do more for that region's tourism than anything else before or since. Shenandoah National Park, in the Blue Ridge Mountains of Virginia, and Great Smoky Mountains National Park, straddling the Tennessee/North Carolina border, would eventually both prove to be great draws for tourists . . . athough, owing to the nature of the National Parks, actual tourism development was concentrated around their periphery rather than within the boundaries of the parks proper.

In 1933, the government conceived of a grand WPA (Works Progress Administration) project: a thoroughfare that would connect the Shenandoah and Great Smoky Mountains parks, simultaneously providing jobs for the well-publicized poverty-stricken inhabitants of Appalachia. In 1936, a year after construction began, this completely new highway was named the Blue Ridge Parkway, and placed under the control of the

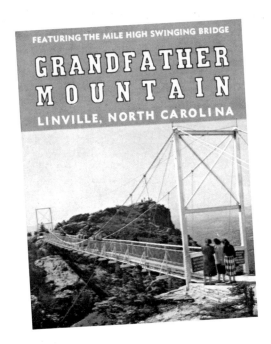

National Park System. The Blue Ridge Parkway, like the National Parks it connected, served to draw motorists to itself . . . and, intentionally or not, birthed a number of roadside attractions along the length of its route. Again, because of its inherently noncommercial nature, most of the Parkway's attractions were simply located "near" the highway.

Since pioneer days, a certain craggy peak near Linville, North Carolina, had been known as "Grandfather Mountain," theoretically because when viewed from the north the mountain's profile resembled an old man looking skyward. Some activity took place around the base of the mountain during the 1880s, but, as with most attractions, things really got busy when someone realized that automobile tourists could be brought in with just a little work. In the early 1900s, entrepreneur Julian Morton widened a preexisting horseback trail into a one-lane highway, constructed a wooden viewing platform, and began charging admission to drive up to the mountain's summit. In 1946, Julian Morton's son Hugh started laying plans to open up Grandfather Mountain to more visitors. He first widened the existing road to two lanes, and by September 2, 1952, Grandfather Mountain was ready to be dedicated to the public. Its chief feature—apart from the terrific view—was its Mile-High Swinging Bridge, no doubt inspired by the very similar structure at Rock City Gardens on Lookout Mountain.

Further down the Blue Ridge Parkway, two relatives of Grandfather Mountain were also built around their preexisting rock formations. Chimney Rock

Park was developed largely by the Morse brothers, Lucius, Hiram, and Asahel, who purchased the property in 1902 with the idea of making it accessible to the general public. A new bridge and road to the Chimney Rock formation itself were opened in 1916, and three years later the park got a restaurant to serve the ever-increasing number of guests. After the usual setback in finances and visitors during the Depression, the postwar world found Chimney Rock constructing an elevator that got a rise out of visitors, whisking them from the parking lot to a spot near the top of the "chimney," from which they could enjoy a marvelous 75-mile view. Chimney Rock Park was eventually joined on the Parkway by Blowing Rock, named so because of the constant wind that could be found there.

One of today's primary attractions off the Blue Ridge Parkway actually started out as anything but that. In 1887 the unbelievably rolling-in-dough George Vanderbilt decided to build a house near Asheville, in the North Carolina mountains. However, calling his creation a house is like calling the Mona Lisa a cartoon character. Biltmore, as the residence was named, contained by the time it was completed in 1895 some 250 rooms (including 32 guest rooms). It featured immaculately landscaped gardens, and the mansion itself was filled with rare and (naturally) expensive art treasures from around the world. According to historians, it was around 1930 that the city of Asheville prevailed upon the Vanderbilt heirs to open portions of their home for tours. After the socialites departed for other climes, the residence became strictly

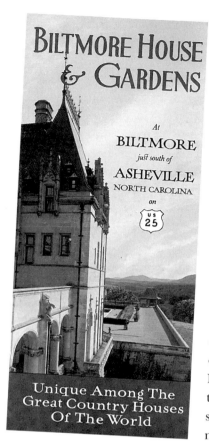

BILTMORE HOUSE & GARDENS

At
BILTMORE
just south of
ASHEVILLE
NORTH CAROLINA
on
US 25

Unique Among The Great Country Houses Of The World

a tourist attraction during the 1960s, giving the general public at least a taste of what that life-style must have been like.

The Blue Ridge Parkway ended in the Great Smoky Mountains National Park. Unlike the others, the Great Smoky Mountains Park was actually brainstormed and created by the states of Tennessee and North Carolina themselves. The two states bought up as much acreage as they could, and once they had it all tied together, they turned it over to the federal government. The process of turning private farmland into a National Park stretched over a period from 1925 to 1940, but by 1934 the park was starting to make a name for itself as a popular vacation destination.

The centerpiece of the Great Smoky Moun-

tains eventually turned out to be the once-sleepy community of Gatlinburg, Tennessee. Like many resort areas, which are generally not known for preserving their past, the easiest thing to explain about Gatlinburg is its name. It was originally called White Oak Flats, and its main business enterprise was a general store owned by one Daniel Reagan. Another character with the last name of Gatlin eventually bought the store, but he then announced that the locals could not pick up their mail at the post office (which was located in the store) unless they renamed their town after him! Hence, Gatlinburg came into being. Even today, legends about Gatlin and his chicanery prevail in the town.

It is slightly more difficult to pinpoint just how the village became the tourist capital that

President Roosevelt officially dedicates the Great Smoky Mountains National Park, 1940.

Head for the Hills

Fireside Candies was an early sweet shop in Gatlinburg, Tennessee.

it is today. Official city histories assert that Gatlinburg's resort status began to germinate when wealthy citizens of Knoxville began using it as a getaway spot in the early 1900s. In 1910, the Pi Beta Phi national sorority adopted Gatlinburg as a project, trying to help the locals make a better life for themselves by establishing schools, medical facilities, and other such citified notions. One of Pi Beta Phi's ideas was to begin selling the furniture and handicrafts that for centuries the mountain

folks had been turning out for their own use, thus giving the people a source of income other than their hardscrabble farms. In 1926 the sorority established a Gatlinburg store, the Arrowcraft Shop, and its surplus crafts were in turn shipped to Pi Beta Phi shops across the country. This served to spread Gatlinburg's reputation as a craft center nationwide.

The years immediately following the Depression saw another handicraft offshoot come to town, with the arrival of the first homemade candy shops. Aunt Mahalia's Candies, cooked up in 1939, currently promotes itself as the oldest goody store in Gatlinburg.

In fact, for many years, crafts and candy were practically the only things to be found in Gatlinburg. Then, once the postwar tourism craze got underway, the town began to expand its horizons a bit. 1951 saw the establishment of Homespun Valley Mountaineer Village, where a working mill, blacksmith shop, moonshine still, and other such attractions gave visitors a look at what pioneer mountain life was all about—more so than viewing tidy little baskets and furniture would have.

What is probably Gatlinburg's oldest non-pioneer-related attraction came into being in 1954, when the Gatlinburg Sky Lift began hauling tourists from street level to the top of Crockett Mountain. Despite its name, which conjures up images of the airborne buckets that carried visitors aloft at such parks as Six Flags Over Georgia, Gatlinburg's Sky Lift was basically a chairlift of the type seen often at ski resorts. In fact, some publicity claimed that it was the first of its type to be installed in the South. This may very well be true, but it is most certainly a fact that it was one of the first chairlifts to *not* be used for skiing facilities!

Another of the more permanent of Gatlinburg's early attractions had its beginning when a young Tennessean, Ronald S. Ligon, contracted a nearly fatal illness. It seems that Ligon's life was spared only through divine intervention, and Ligon determined to show his gratitude by establishing a permanent memorial to the life of Christ. Gatlinburg was chosen as the site of his tribute because of its natural beauty, and also because it was rapidly becoming the tourist center of that part of the state.

Ligon had no interest in building a dinky little roadside dime museum. He commissioned a Toronto display firm to design his dioramas, which were then executed by a London, England, company known as Gems Ltd. The wax figures were augmented with human hair and realistic eyes, and clothed in costumes created by B. J. Simmons Ltd., the same company that had designed the wardrobes for the famous Biblical movies *Ben Hur* and *Quo Vadis*. Ligon's new Christus Gardens opened on August 13, 1960.

GATLINBURG'S

Christus Gardens

CHRISTUS GARDENS, AN OUTSTANDING ALL-YEAR, ALL-WEATHER ATTRACTION

OGLE'S TWIN ISLANDS MOTEL & CAFE GATLINBURG TENNESSEE

Where the Eleet sleep and eat!

One of many Smoky Mountain businesses to employ the stereotypical hillbilly image.

Head fer the Hills

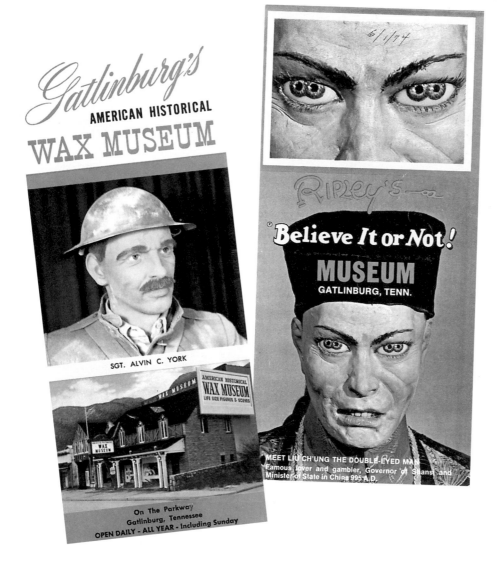

Gatlinburg's AMERICAN HISTORICAL WAX MUSEUM

SGT. ALVIN C. YORK

AMERICAN HISTORICAL WAX MUSEUM LIFE SIZE FIGURES & SCENES

On The Parkway
Gatlinburg, Tennessee
OPEN DAILY - ALL YEAR - Including Sunday

Ripley's
Believe It or Not!
MUSEUM
GATLINBURG, TENN.

MEET LIU CH'UNG THE DOUBLE-EYED MAN
Famous lover and gambler, Governor of Shansi and
Minister of State in China 995 A.D.

The entire life of Christ, from the Nativity to the Ascension, was depicted in Christus Gardens' dioramas, complete with dramatic lighting, sound effects, and specially recorded chorale music. The site definitely accomplished its purpose of being a serene and inspiring alternative to the hullabaloo of the rest of the mountain resort. However, the expression "success breeds imitation" is demonstrated nowhere better than in the tourism industry, so it should come as no surprise that Christus Gardens soon found itself unequally yoked with yet another Biblical-themed attraction . . . sort of.

In the mid-1960s, an anonymous entrepreneur who let himself be known only as "the Chaplain" apparently decided that since Christus Gardens was doing such a magnificent job in depicting the beauty of Christ's life, perhaps he could draw in his own share of visitors by giving them—how shall we put this delicately?—the "other side" of the Bible. With this thought in mind, the Chaplain's contribution to the tourists' religious edification was called—are you ready for this?—the Tour Through Hell.

In all the world there could be no better description of Gatlinburg's Tour Through Hell than its own lurid publicity release: "The Chaplain's Tour Through Hell is a tour through a rocklike structure with deep winding caves. You will thrill at the many interesting things to be seen, such as the Lake of Fire, and Pontius Pilate's hands turning to blood before your very eyes. This is one of the most educational tourist attractions anywhere, and is based on Biblical facts. The cavelike passageways glow like they are red hot, and provide the lighting system for the tour. You'll actually walk on the Burning Brimstone. You'll actually see an Invisible Hand with the drop of water floating in the air, which the rich man in the 16th Chapter of Luke prayed for. This idea originally came from a sermon the Chaplain preached many times. The Chaplain believes that this attraction will be most interesting and fascinating, as well as educational and instructive."

An Invisible Hand? Now *there's* a low-budget special effect for you! (Tour Guide: "Look, there's the Invisible Hand! Do you see it?" Tourist: "No." Guide: "Well of course not, it's invisible!!") But enough about that. It probably says something good about human nature that Christus Gardens still thrives today, while the Tour Through Hell was soon sent straight to . . . aw, you get the idea.

Another mid-1960s Gatlinburg attraction that took the diorama angle in a more secular direction was the American Historical Wax Museum, somewhat appropriately housed in the town's former movie theatre. Here were shown some 45 scenes from American history, from the Declaration of Independence to the assassination of Lee Harvey Oswald. (Apparently this museum wanted to mix the inspiration of Christus Gardens with the shock value of the Tour Through Hell.)

When it comes to shock value, however, the Gatlinburg wax museum to end all wax museums poured ino town in 1969 with the opening of the Ripley's Believe It Or Not Museum. This attraction does at least have a lengthy lineage that keeps it from being a simple get-rich-quick scheme. Cartoonist Robert L. Ripley created his *Believe It Or Not* newspaper feature in 1918. He soon parlayed its success into books, radio, motion pictures, television, and temporary exhibits at various World's Fairs. After Ripley's death in 1949, his company, Ripley International, continued the production of the newspaper cartoons and began establishing a series of permanent museums to exhibit parts of their large collections.

A Ripley's Museum had already been operating in St. Augustine, Florida, for nearly twenty years before the Gatlinburg "Odditorium" was established (see chapter 6). At the time, the company gave the following answer when asked why Gatlinburg had been chosen for their newest site: "No matter in what media it has been presented, Ripley's Believe It Or Not has always been particularly well received by people below the Mason-Dixon Line. To situate a museum in an area where a great percentage of our fans originate seemed the logical thing to do."

The location may have been the only logical thing about Ripley's Museum, and probably the late cartoonist himself would have delighted in the fact. Many of the exhibits were actual items from the Ripley archives, but others were simply reproductions of such items. The two were not always differentiated. The advertising for the museum put great emphasis on its recreation of one Liu Ch'ung, an ancient minister of state in China. The honorable Mr. Ch'ung was notable because he had two pupils in his eyes. This would be normal for anyone, except that our friend here had two pupils in *each* eye, for a grand total of four. His undeniably startling visage graced the Gatlinburg Ripley's ads for many years.

The original location of Ripley's Gatlinburg museum was heavily damaged by a fire in 1992, and after being out of commission for nearly three years, in 1995 it reopened in a much larger three-story building, bedecked with a leaning tower that appeared to be ready to crumble onto the sidewalk below at any second. In another true illustration of the "imita-

The Space Needle was Gatlinburg's entry in the great observation tower craze of the 1960s.

tion/flattery" observation, since Ripley's debut Gatlinburg has become inundated with macabre exhibits stressing the horrific, bizarre, and just plain weird.

Not all of Gatlinburg's attractions were promoted with such fiendish glee. Mystery Hill, for example, was one of those "trick houses" that hearkened back to the good old innocent days of roadside travel. "Here the law of gravity seems to have gone berserk," their ads read, "and your sense of balance is entirely upset." Actually, of course, the sense of balance was upset when the attraction's various optical illusions were devised, but it could still be a pleasant diversion. The only thing that was never explained was how Mystery Hill could be separated by only a wooden fence from the large miniature golf course next door, yet the strange things that happened at Mystery Hill were not in evidence less than five feet away. Now *that* is a truly perplexing paradox!

A short-lived Gatlinburg attraction that could only be described as "of its own time" was the (then) futuristic-looking "Space Ship." Built along the same steamlined lines as Disneyland's Rocket to Mars, Gatlinburg's Space Ship advertised, "There's no need to delay your trip to outer space. A space ship leaves Gatlinburg on regular schedules for the moon and points beyond. Vacationing astronauts hear the countdown, break the sound barrier, and think they look back upon Earth from orbit." Apparently the landing of *real* astronauts on the moon at the end of the 1960s put such hokey science fiction features out of business, but they were tacky fun while they lasted.

With the passion for observation towers that swept tourist centers in the 1960s and 1970s, it is not surprising that Gatlinburg made its own entry in the high and mighty category. The 342-foot Space Needle, which did bear a vague resemblance to its Seattle, Washington, namesake, opened in May 1970. Like most observation towers, it offered little but a trip to the top in an elevator, but its view of the Great Smoky Mountains was unparalleled. All too typically, by the 1990s that was considered definitely hohum stuff, and the base of the Space Needle brought forth arcade games, a virtual reality center, a playground, and other less-than-serene activities.

If Gatlinburg was the "Gateway to the Great Smoky Mountains," as it was touted, then there was another town that served as the "Gateway to Gatlinburg." A few miles north, on U.S. 441, was Pigeon Forge. Today's histories of the town's tourism development usually begin with the early 1980s, and for good reason. Prior to that time, Pigeon Forge was looked upon as Gatlinburg's poor barefoot cousin . . . and not even a kissin' cousin at that! In fact, a 1954 souvenir map of the Great Smokies failed to include even a dot representing the then insignificant community.

As a town (not as the tourist hot spot it is today), Pigeon Forge had its beginnings around 1781, long before there was even a state of Tennessee. The first structure in what would eventually become Pigeon Forge was a fort built by one Col. Samuel Wear. The name "Pigeon Forge" came from the community's iron works, which were located on the Little Pigeon River.

Establishment of the National Park brought tourists to Pigeon Forge for the first time, but even then it did not immediately become a beehive of activity. Pigeon Forge Pottery, which still draws visitors today, was established in 1946, but it was not particularly the start of a trend. As late as 1959, the only other attraction listed in the town was the Fort Weare Game Park.

Named after the original fort built by Samuel Wear (and probably adding the final "e" to the name to distinguish the two), Fort Weare Game Park was described thus: "Here you may see a large and interesting collection of animals, birds, and reptiles . . . elephants, bears, tigers, lions, pumas, deer, elk, monkeys by the dozen, and a Cherokee Indian village." It was contained within a structure made to resemble somewhat the original Fort Wear.

More attractions began nesting in Pigeon Forge during the 1960s. Some of these are covered in other chapters, under other subjects, such as Fairyland and Magic World (see

Ft. Weare Game Park was one of the first tourist attractions in Pigeon Forge, Tenn.

chapter 5) and the various incarnations of the Rebel Railroad (see chapter 9). Another arrival of the period was the Hillbilly Museum, which eventually grew and grew into what is today known as Hill-Billy Village (the hyphen is theirs). The original museum was promoted as "The MOST educational attraction in the Smokies, featuring thousands of primitive early American antiques." Hill-Billy Village is the quintessential Smoky Mountains tourist trap—and that is not a derogatory term—with its painted wall murals of moonshine-drinkin', shotgun-totin' mountaineers and Daisy Mae lookalikes. The museum angle is still present, with exhibits of split rail fences, log cabins, and stills, but the complex now includes every variety of craft shop, candy kitchen, and snack bar as well.

In its quest for a position in the lucrative tourism industry, Pigeon Forge even tried subscribing to the mania for the porpoise shows made famous by Marineland and other such Florida locales. The Tennessee Porpoise Circus may well have been one of the most out-of-place attractions in the whole Southern mountains, as very few porpoises can be found swimming around the hazy hills of the Great Smokies. Another transplant was the Smoky Mountain Car Museum, which simply continued the tradition begun further south by Cars of Yesterday in Sarasota, Florida, and the Carriage Cavalcade and Early American Museum at Silver Springs (see chapter 6).

In 1965, li'l ole Pigeon Forge had only four restaurants, two drive-ins, and ten motels (whose combined rooms would accommodate a grand total of 250), but within a decade it began to beat its chest and yell, letting everyone know it was there. The tourist boom really hit Pigeon Forge around 1981–82, making it probably one of the last tourist centers to reach its full potential. Actually, one cause for this was probably that Gatlinburg's narrow roadways were about to choke on their own success, and there was literally nowhere else to build anything new in that town. The arrival of the huge Dollywood theme park in the space that had operated under several different attraction names since 1961 was a major spark plug in Pigeon Forge's newfound drawing power. Today, miniature golf courses, weird attractions, restaurants, and motels, motels, motels line Pigeon Forge's four-lane U.S. 441, obliterating the community's original appearance. But no one seems to care, as those almighty tourist dollars are great for drying the tears of any overly concerned historians.

With both Gatlinburg and Pigeon Forge mining the hillbilly image for all it was worth, a trip across the Smokies into North Carolina could be like entering another world altogether. On this eastern side of the mountains, bears remained but hillbillies disappeared, only to be replaced by an American Indian motif in an even more pervasive way.

At least it can be said that this Indian theme had authentic roots. Cherokee, North Carolina, serves as the center of an actual reservation, and it too benefited from the arrival of the National Park. Perhaps inspired by what was going on across the hills in Gatlinburg, during the 1940s the reservation's inhabitants began directing their centuries-old traditions toward the tourist trade.

Authentic recreations of Cherokee life could best be seen at the Oconaluftee Indian Village, established in 1951. Here was a full-size replica of a circa 1750 village, with true Native Americans demonstrating their artistry at feathering arrows, fashioning blow guns, chipping flint into arrowheads, carving wooden spoons and other utensils, and pounding corn into meal with a mortar and pestle. There were also demonstrations of canoe-building, stringing beads, mold-

ing ropes of clay into pots, weaving baskets, and finger-weaving cloth. Near the Oconaluftee Village was the live outdoor drama *Unto These Hills,* depicting the history of the Cherokee Nation. (It will be covered in chapter 6, along with other such historical plays.)

Such real-life exhibits were, and remain, invaluable documentation of the true history of the Cherokee people. However, as the crowds of tourists grew larger and larger, the town of Cherokee found itself drifting more and more into a "commercial" version of Indian life, at least so far as the attractions and shops along its two main thoroughfares, U.S. 441 and U.S. 19, were concerned. An example of this is the preponderance of tepees, or wigwams, which were never used by any Indian tribe except the nomadic peoples of the Western plains. The Plains Indians were also to thank for the image of the elaborately-feathered Indian headdress, which likewise turned up around every corner in Cherokee. Totem poles were another element not employed by the Cherokees until the palefaces came to town. However, all of these emblems

The Cherokees adopted such non-native props as tepees and feathered headdresses and learned to accept plastic wampum for having their photos taken.

spelled "Indian" to the tourists who were weaned on Western movies and TV series, so the real-life Cherokees had no qualms about adopting them.

The mid-1960s saw the debut of another historical-themed attraction, but one that took a completely different approach than the Oconaluftee Village and its latter-day papooses. At the Cyclorama of the Cherokee Indian, a series of life-sized dioramas depicted important scenes from Cherokee history via the tourism-happy medium of wax figures. Some of these scenes were even illuminated by that age-old favorite effect, black light, which gave them the appearance of overgrown escapees from Rock City Gardens' Fairyland Caverns. (Back in Gatlinburg, Indian history was being played out at the Cherokee-Rama, which did its storytelling with hundreds of tiny figures on a huge landscape, much like Chattanooga's similarly-named Confederama.)

Not all attractions in Cherokee used the Indian theme...just most of them. In chapter 5 we will visit Santa's Land, where jolly old Kris Kringle set up his workshop for the summer among the peaks of the Smokies. Chapter 9 will include the Western-themed Frontier Land, which did feature Indians, but in a totally non-North Carolina setting.

One of the most bizarre non-Indian ventures was the Mystery House, which was a contemporary of the Mystery Hill we have already seen in Gatlinburg. The Mystery House, however, employed a much more sensationalistic approach: "The Mystery House has thwarted all attempts to explain the weird power that exists within and about it," the publicity shouted. "This is a natural mystery...no tricks...nor mirrors...nothing moving. Even the one who designed it can't explain it." Right. Probably what the designer couldn't explain was why such museums of optical illusions kept bringing in the customers for so many years. But they did, and while the Mystery House and Mystery Hill are no longer with us, it does make one wonder what strange phenomena the businesses who occupy their former sites might be dealing with now....

Though Lookout Mountain was somewhat separated from the rest of the continuous string of Appalachian resorts, it did not come up short when it came to contributing attractions to the South's mountain tourism. Rock City and Ruby Falls, of course, are thoroughly covered in chapter 7, but in our discussion of the mountains, the peak of Lookout itself deserves closer examination here.

Lookout Mountain's reputation as a summer resort was established even before the Civil War. Its strategic location made it a prize piece of ground during that war, and history books have well related the many battles that were fought to claim it. What has not been recorded so thoroughly, though, is that between battles the military personnel stationed on the mountain found time to write of its wonders in their personal diaries. A Union soldier and a Confederate nurse, writing separately, both noted that the view from the top of Lookout was unbelievable. "It is said," they wrote, "that seven states can be seen on a clear day." This slogan soon became attached to the unusual outcropping named Umbrella Rock (due to its shape), but it would eventually be picked up and made famous by Rock City during the 1930s and 1940s.

As in the other mountainous regions, transportation up Lookout Mountain was sometimes hazardous. The only roads were crooked and unpaved, and the mountain's steep grades made ascension a risky adventure. This problem was at least partly alleviated in 1887 with the construction of the first Incline railway up the mountain. This original Incline had its share of financial problems, and in 1895 a second Incline was built to replace it. This is the one that is still giving visitors a new slant on Lookout Mountain today.

Actually, the Incline was not originally intended as a tourism piece. Its purpose was practical: to get people from Chattanooga to the top of Lookout in the most direct manner

possible. In fact, while it is now promoted heavily in Chattanooga's tourist industry, the Incline remains legally a piece of the city's public transit system, and is heavily used by those who have to commute from their mountaintop homes to jobs in the city each day.

Advertised as "America's Most Amazing Mile," the two Incline cars travel up and down Lookout's slopes at a speed of eight miles per hour. Counterbalanced like the buckets in a well, as one car moves down the other is pulled up. Both travel upon the same track, except at the spot where they pass in the middle of the trip, at which there is a double set of tracks. Like any good tourist attraction, the upper and lower Incline station houses contain an assortment of souvenir shops and snack bars.

For those who still preferred to drive up Lookout Mountain, a new paved highway was opened in April 1927. A newspaper article of the time reported that "the motoring public will find the new road much easier to travel and 100% safer than the old road. More than 50% of the curves have been eliminated, and those that have been retained have been made much easier to take by elevation of the road some 18 inches on the outer side of all curves." For anyone who has made the winding, twisting journey to the mountain top, the thought of the old highway being even more crooked is a gut-wrenching idea indeed!

Improved highways brought with them a new boom for Lookout. Lavish luxury hotels flourished, and within a few years the Incline was joined by fellow attractions Rock City and Ruby Falls. But as the number of out-of-town visitors increased, a somewhat seedy enterprise grew up around the mountain's base. Travelers found themselves faced with small booths labeled "Lookout Mountain Guides." These guides especially preyed upon cars with flatlands license plates: they would tell horror stories of how treacherous the mountain's roads could be, and their histrionics were convincing enough to talk many tourists into shelling out several bucks to pay the guides to drive their cars for them.

Besides these questionable tactics, the guides were also involved in a sort of moblike protection business. Rock City, Ruby Falls, and their pals paid the guides a percentage of their profits; in exchange the guides drove the tourists' cars to their gates. In the late 1930s, Rock City founder Garnet Carter announced that he would no longer pay commissions to the guides, and nearly started what newspapers called the "Second Battle of Lookout Mountain." Soon the entire Chattanooga tourism industry was involved, everyone taking sides either with the guides or with Carter. The whole mess was never totally resolved, but the advent of World War II and the resulting disintegration of the tourist business must have settled the guides' hash once and for all, because practically nothing regarding them was recorded after the conflict ended.

Today it is difficult to say whether the Southern mountains or the Southern beaches are the most popular. While both fall firmly into the tourist attraction category, they approach this genre in differing ways. While the beaches continually strive for a more teenager-oriented look, the mountains perhaps aim themselves more at the family trade. There are exceptions to these rules in each region, however, so it is safe to say that both destinations will continue to hold their own in future years. They continue to illustrate that incredible variety that is available below the Mason-Dixon Line!

Fantasy Lands

To please a child is a sweet and lovely thing that warms one's heart and brings its own reward.

—L. Frank Baum

Even after the development of the South's beaches and mountain regions was well underway, there was one more major event that had to take place to bring tourist attractions to their full fruition. For the first three decades of automobile tourism, not much thought had been given to the children who might be accompanying their parents. Attraction owners and others in the industry had concentrated on selling to adults, going to any lengths to persuade them to stop the car and spend some time (and, not incidentally, money).

All of that changed in the years immediately following World War II. The returning soldiers were anxious to get married and start families, and this resulted in what became known as the postwar "baby boom." The boom created an infantry of children who would be taking their places in the family sedan, and it didn't take long for the tourism industry to realize that these pint-sized promoters could be valuable allies. The new goal was getting the *kids* to be the ones who nagged their parents to stop!

One of the first attractions in the South to begin its courtship of the travelers' children was Rock City Gardens. In 1947 they put a roof over a long crevice in the rocks, and named the resulting artificial cave "Fairyland Caverns." Fairyland Caverns was populated by the colorful creations of sculptor Jessie Sanders, all illuminated by glowing, ultraviolet "black light." Most of these depicted scenes from the famous stories that have been beloved for hundreds of years: Little Red Riding Hood was caught in deep discussion with a certain wolf; Jack chopped away at a beanstalk as an ugly giant fee-fi-fo-fummed his way down the vine; Rip Van Winkle was bowled over by a gang of elfin tenpin players. Snow White and all seven dwarfs (*not* the Disney versions) went through several different incarnations before Sanders hit upon an arrangement that seemed right to her. Also included were original scenes not taken from any story, such as the "Dream Fairies" diorama, with its multicolored sprites floating through the bedroom window of two sleeping kids.

The success of Fairyland Caverns was so

complete that Rock City unveiled a companion piece, Mother Goose Village, in May 1964. This time, all of the scenes from the timeless nursery rhymes were displayed in a huge landscape topped by a ten-foot-tall castle. The cow really did jump over the moon, Contrary Mary watered her garden as Humpty Dumpty egged her on, and kindly old Mother Goose herself (depicted as a real goose instead of as an elderly woman) kept watch over it all.

Fairyland Caverns' charming appeal to both young and old sent shock waves through the tourist industry. Soon it seemed that anyone with a knack for sculpture and a place to display their artistry began creating fairy tale scenes, and the beautiful thing was that, since the old folk tales were not copyrighted, they were open to anyone and everyone's interpretation. Thus it was that in the early 1960s, en route to Pigeon Forge, Tennessee, tourists found themselves besieged with billboards advertising that town's "Fabulous Fairyland!"

No manmade cavern this, Pigeon Forge's Fairyland was contained within a houselike building surrounded by kiddie boat rides, a merry-go-round, picnic grounds, and the obligatory gift shop. But once inside, Fairyland's inspiration became crystal clear. Again visitors were treated to various fairy tale tableaux illuminated by black light. The main difference was that the figures in Pigeon Forge's Fairyland

were mechanically animated, while those in Fairyland Caverns were immobile. The Pigeon Forge figures were also much smaller, so many more of them were crowded into what turned out to be a relatively small space. For those too old to appreciate Red Riding Hood, Mother Goose, and their compadres, the Fairyland owners also displayed their collection of antique guns. This undoubtedly left many people continuing their vacation with one thought burning in their minds: "What did antique guns have to do with fairy tales?"

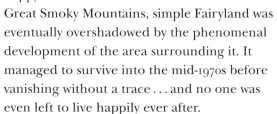

Although advertised heavily during the years when Pigeon Forge was first trying to find its niche in the tourist-happy world of the Great Smoky Mountains, simple Fairyland was eventually overshadowed by the phenomenal development of the area surrounding it. It managed to survive into the mid-1970s before vanishing without a trace . . . and no one was even left to live happily ever after.

Still another Fairyland danced merrily into

being in Tampa, Florida, a pet project of that city's mayor, Nick C. Nuccio. Located in Lowry Park, Fairyland of Tampa bore less resemblance to the others than might be expected. The fact that it was outdoors had a lot to do with it, as for once black light was not being used. Fifteen acres were transformed into what one of their promotional brochures described as "a unique fantasyland appealing to all ages. In addition to life-size portrayals of fables and fairy tales, there is a free playground with slides, swings, and seesaws, a real Navy plane, a fire engine, and a zoo with regularly scheduled animal performances." The place also featured a miniature golf course that fell firmly into the concrete-dinosaur category popularized in the late 1950s. Defying time and the changes it inevitably brings with it, Tampa's Fairyland still stands in Lowry Park today, although it has been renamed the Fun Forest.

If comedian Jimmy Durante had been studying children's tourist attractions at the time, he would have uttered his famous quote, "Everybody wants ta get inta da act!" Even attractions that had never thought about such things before could be found grafting fantasy themes onto their existing property. Florida's Cypress Gardens, never noted for its tot appeal, incorporated "Fantasy Valley" into the regular tour in 1965, with giant statues representing various tales. Over in Tampa, Busch Gardens brewed up "Dwarf Village," with still more outdoor dioramas of Hansel and Gretel, Snow White, and various fairyland flora and fauna.

Meanwhile, in the South's hill country, North Carolina's Tweetsie Railroad had been a typical Western-town attraction, but during the

Tweetsie Railroad's Castle of the Sleeping Giant.

fantasy land heyday they added the Castle of the Sleeping Giant. The snoring behemoth kept up a reign of terror in his mountaintop fortress for many years, but the castle has now fallen into disrepair and is no longer a part of the Tweetsie complex. The Children's Zoo of Roanoke, Virginia, went after a Mother Goose theme, with a giant walk-through shoe and fairytale castle, among other elements.

While all of these places were toying with the Fairyland concept, up on Beech Mountain, near Banner Elk, North Carolina, another type of fairyland was about to take shape. It seems that Beech Mountain's economy depended heavily upon its winter ski trade, and in 1969 North Carolina tourism tycoons Grover and Harry Robbins set out to find some sort of lure that would draw people to the mountaintop during the summer months.

Jack Pentes, a designer from Charlotte, was enlisted to examine the property and come up with an idea. Pentes later recalled, "I walked among that long-stemmed emerald grass, a vivid green that I had never seen before. The trees grabbed me, those beautiful trees that couldn't be anywhere else . . . except for the feeling that I had seen them before. Their limbs seemed to be reaching out for me. Then, rounding the face of a small pinnacle, I saw a small cave. That is where it was, I think, that I

Spook Hill in Lake Wales, Florida, may have had the most low-budget fantasy characters in history. Cars appeared to roll uphill, pulled by (invisible) ghosts.

realized, 'This is the Land of Oz! The Cowardly Lion's cave is even where it's supposed to be!'"

The version of the Land of Oz that finally landed on this side of the rainbow was, in fact, based partially on the famous 1939 movie starring Judy Garland, partially on the original Oz stories by L. Frank Baum, and partially on Pentes' own imagination. Lending authenticity to the park was the presence of Ray Bolger, the Scarecrow of Oz himself, at the groundbreaking ceremonies. At the entrance to the attraction was their pride and joy, a museum containing several original props and costumes from the movie, along with early editions of the Baum books.

Visitors first came upon the turn-of-the-century farm of Uncle Henry and Aunt Em, touring the farmhouse, which was furnished with appropriate period antiques. Being told that a cyclone was on the horizon, the crowd was then herded into the storm cellar, a darkened maze of wind and sound effects. Arriving back upstairs, visitors found what appeared to be the same farmhouse, only tilted several degrees in two directions, with the fur-niture a total wreck. This, of course, was a second house connected to the first by the cellar maze.

From that point, the whole saga of the wonderful Wizard of Oz played itself out. Traveling a real yellow brick road, visitors encountered the Scarecrow, the Tin Woodman, and the Cowardly Lion, and eluded the clutches of the bumbling Wicked Witch. The visit climaxed at the Emerald City, with a live stage show in which the characters' wishes were all granted. (In this pageant, the Wizard was not revealed as a humbug, a major change from the original story and subsequent movie.)

Apparently the Wicked Witch and her flying monkeys finally decided to get their revenge on the Land of Oz, because on December 28, 1975, the attraction suffered two major blows. Practically everything in the museum was stolen during a break-in, while a fire swept through the Emerald City, doing even more irreparable harm. Things were never quite the same in Oz after that, and it limped along through some mighty lean years, finally closing after its 1980 operating season. During the ten years that followed, vandals almost succeeded in decimating what was left of the abandoned park, but in 1990 the property was purchased to be used as a residential development known as Emerald Mountain. The surviving pieces of Oz were carefully preserved as a sort of private garden; the Emerald City is gone, but Dorothy's house and the Yellow Brick Road have been restored to their original storybook splendor. As Emerald Mountain reports, "The park is not, nor will it ever be, what it once was. However, with its maturing flora and graceful aging, it has evolved into its own unique entity."

If there were a kid alive who did not care to visit the Land of Oz, perhaps Santa Claus's workshop at the North Pole would be more to their liking. Christmas-themed attractions had already been an incongruous part of summer vacations in other parts of the country for several years when Cherokee, North Carolina, debuted "Santa's Land" in 1966. Drawn in by the towering St. Nick at the entrance, tourists were engulfed in a Yuletide world that looked bizarrely out of place against the background of the Smokies' wooded hillsides.

Santa's house was there, of course, complete with the jolly old man himself and his waiting lap. It is not recorded how many children were actually thinking about what they wanted for Christmas in the middle of the summer. An Eskimo igloo, complete with penguin, made a vain attempt to look cool and frosty in the sweltering heat. The blacksmith shop starred a real-life smithy, plying his trade as in years gone by. A one-room schoolhouse and a post office (with its own Santa's Land postmark) were also included in the tour. Not to ignore the other side of Christmas, a large, beautifully crafted nativity scene occupied a quiet corner of the property. Oddly, the items in Santa's Souvenir Shop were actually sold for money, even though we all thought Kris Kringle always *gave* his presents away!

There was a time when simple attractions such as Santa's Land provided thrills enough to satisfy any kid. But, as they say, "that was then and this is now." Like Santa's waistline, Santa's Land continued growing as the years passed. While other fantasy attractions faded and disappeared, Santa's Land kept adding more and more features until today the original part of the park (known as "Santa's Village") takes up only one microscopic sliver of the whole. Amusement park rides, including the red-nosed "Rudi-Coaster," and a complete zoo filled the rest of the property.

In keeping with the evergreen philosophy that truth is stranger than fiction, some attractions eschewed the fairy tale concept and went straight to realism of the most fantastic kind . . . namely, dinosaurs. These lumbering creatures combined the most bizarre appearances possible with the underlying knowledge that they actually did exist at

Fantasy Lands

Bongoland's concrete dinosaurs retain their primitive charm even today.

Virginia's Dinosaur Land as it appeared shortly after its opening. The trees have now taken over the landscape.

one time. Their universal appeal gave birth to another whole genre of fantasy-themed destinations.

One of the first Southern attractions to employ dinosaurs was Bongoland, an amusement park in Daytona Beach. Originally a botanical garden, Bongoland received its new name in 1946 when the owner began displaying a trained baboon named Bongo at the entrance. Bongo's job was to greet the visitors and pick their pockets, and the public went ape over him. Although practically forgotten today, Bongoland evolved into a primitive version of a theme park, with "Spanish ruins and an Indian village," as Florida writer Jack Kofoed described it, and a remarkable collection of concrete dinosaur statues. Today, Bongoland has reverted to its original form and is known as Sugar Mill Gardens, but the dinosaurs can still be seen in all their Mesozoic glory.

Another stomping ground for concrete critters was Dinosaur Land, located just north of Shenandoah National Park at White Post, Virginia. The attraction's founder, Joseph Geraci, was quite taken with some dino work done in

Florida and in Gatlinburg by reptile resurrector Jim Sidwell, and commissioned Sidwell to bring his talents to the northern Virginia hills. Dinosaur Land opened around 1965, with a miscellaneous collection of outdoor prehistoric dioramas. The attraction still brings in brontosaurus fanciers today.

Meanwhile, just north of Bushnell, Florida, on U.S. Highway 301, there sprouted the Rainforest. Here intrepid explorers could traverse forested pathways and encounter still more giant animated dinosaurs lurking in the jungles. Also on the premises was the Sacred Art Garden, featuring "a new medium of art painted in glass, gold, silver, brass, lahn, and mother of pearl." The attraction's literature claimed that "the construction of the art is so different that art critics have not yet coined a word to describe it." We wonder if they ever did. Anyway, apparently all of this was not quite exciting enough, because by 1970 the only thing left of the Rainforest was a

weed-infested parking lot, with a solitary dinosaur standing guard over a boarded-up administration building. Today the Rainforest's property is the site of a country club.

Dinosaurs eventually took up residence more successfully on the South's elaborate miniature golf courses. Miniature golf was itself a Southern invention, originating at the Fairyland Inn on Lookout Mountain in 1925. Future Rock City founder Garnet Carter is usually credited with tying together some preexisting concepts from across the country to create miniature golf in its modern-day form. Carter's chain of courses was known as Tom Thumb Golf, and emphasized the "miniature" part of the name of the game. Tiny houses and elfin statuary were mass-produced to populate the Tom Thumb courses. Carter's version of miniature golf played its last hole when the Great Depression hit, only to be reborn in the postwar baby boom.

The postwar courses were, in one aspect, the polar opposite of the Tom Thumb idea. Now the statuary and obstacles became deliberately oversized, towering over the players. This "concrete dinosaur" style (also known as "dinosaur and windmill") had its beginning in 1958, when Lee Koplin of Panama City Beach opened his first Goofy Golf course. This course was designed to be almost a theme park itself. At the entrance there was even a sign reading,

"This is the MAGIC WORLD, where the ages of time abide in a garden of serenity with perpetual peace and harmony." Passing by on the highway, it took close examination to discern that it was a miniature golf course at all. The landscape was dominated by a towering replica of the Sphinx and a giant chimpanzee clutching an artificial palm tree. The clubhouse was fronted by an enormous sea monster with jagged teeth. The grounds were dotted with figures that, while not actually obstacles in the game, helped add to the otherworldly atmosphere of the place. Golfers were routed across bridges, through thick "jungles" of actual plant growth, and, at one point, forced to navigate a long concrete cave eerily illuminated by that fantasy land favorite, black light.

Goofy Golf of Fort Walton Beach, Florida, 1959.

Goofy Golf spread rapidly. Two more courses, one in Fort Walton Beach and one in Pensacola, were opened in 1959. Today, Goofy Golf can be found throughout the South, and its influence on the look of miniature golf courses is unquestioned. Along the Gulf Coast, this inspiration manifested itself in such courses as Panama

The 1960 Zoo-Land Golf of Panama City Beach has now been demolished to make room for an RV park.

The entrance to the now-extinct Magic World in Pigeon Forge, Tennessee, was marked by a towering concrete volcano.

City Beach's Zoo-Land Golf, built by L. L. Sowell in 1960, Beacon Golf (1961), and Pirate's Cove Golf (1972), all of which have since been demolished for more current (and less appealing) commercial possibilities. Up in Gatlinburg, Tennessee, Jim Sidwell (who would later sculpt saurian statues for Virginia's Dinosaur Land) opened the dinosaur-laden Jolly Golf in 1961; in the 1990s, the name would be altered to Dinosaur Golf, capitalizing on Sidwell's specialty. Similar fantastic designs could be found at Castle Park Golf (Ft. Lauderdale, Fla.), Magic Carpet Golf (Key West and Fort Walton Beach, Fla.), Wacky Golf (Myrtle Beach, S.C., and Jacksonville Beach, Fla.), Jockey's Ridge Golf (Nags Head, N.C.), Spooky Golf (Gulf Shores, Ala.), and Holiday Golf (Daytona Shores, Fla.). Many of these courses were built and owned by the same individuals, often operating under more than one company name.

Then there was the case of Sir Goony Golf, based in Chattanooga, Tennessee. Goony Golf began operations in 1960, and besides the similarity of the names, many of the figures that appeared at all Goony Golf courses were bla-

tant, simplified imitations of sculptures first created for the original Goofy Golf in Panama City Beach. Sir Goony continues its franchising today; Lee Koplin died in 1988, but his son Randy keeps the family tradition alive by building new Goofy Golf courses, using his dad's original figure designs.

While concrete dinosaurs were making tracks across the South's miniature golf courses, their thumping success was too great to be ignored by the rest of the tourist industry (the demise of the Rainforest notwithstanding). Jolly Golf impresario and Dinosaur Land veteran Jim

Sidwell jumped feet first into the saurian sweepstakes by building an attraction of his own known as Magic World in Pigeon Forge, Tennessee. (According to Pigeon Forge city records, Sidwell's antediluvian world actually began life as yet another elaborate miniature golf course.) Magic World featured more prehistoric creatures than the La Brea tar pits, all situated within an area encircled by the ridges of a towering artificial volcano, more than likely inspired by the one found at Panama City Beach's Jungle Land.

The "Volcano Walk" was the original centerpiece of Magic World. Guests tramped through the musty passageways of the concrete mountain, confronted at every turn by spooky sights. The Abominable Snowman hung out in the volcano's depths, as did, inexplicably, the Invisible Man. In one grotto, a skeleton lay on the floor while his ghost, that of an old gold miner, dug away at the wall (well, what do you know, a prospector's specter!). The underground trip climaxed with a journey on the Earth Auger, a compartment inside a rotating drum that gave riders the sensation of turning around and around as the Edgar Rice Burroughs-inspired craft burrowed deep into the center of the earth.

Outside, in the fresh air, passengers could board the Dragon Train for a perilous ride through dinosaur-infested territory. Betraying their common ownership, the dinosaur statues were duplicates of the ones seen at Jolly Golf. The train ride was promoted as "an educational museum of prehistoric life," but education went right out the window once the train entered a tunnel near the end of the ride. Here could be seen gigantic snakes, insects, and other oversized vermin, the likes of which never existed on the face of this earth. Their motionless appearance only served to render the audiotaped sound effects of agonized human screams and groans more laughable.

However, Magic World's dinosaur angle became extinct as the years passed. In the ongoing belief that "more is better," the attraction expanded its coverage to the point that almost nothing was left of the original. Everything from haunted castles to flying saucers to thrill rides to a complete Arabian kingdom eventually filled the property, making whatever dinosaurs happened to be left look dull and stodgy by comparison. Even too much proved not to be enough; after its 1995 operating season, Magic World took a bow and disappeared.

Six Flags founder Angus Wynne, surrounded by some swampland friends.

(Top) Stuckey's candy and souvenir shops were by far the element that most definitely spelled "the South" to tourists from other parts of the country.

(Bottom) The Sea Dip Motel in Daytona Beach, Florida, was a terrific example of what might be termed the Jetsons Style of architecture of the 1960s.

As indicated by this vintage magazine ad, the Horne's restaurants and candy stores were primarily located along major tourist routes to Florida.

(Top) The Ozark Mountains of northern Arkansas were that state's most famous tourist region for many years.

(Bottom) After the Great Smoky Mountains became a national park in the 1930s, such tourist meccas as Gatlinburg, Pigeon Forge, and Cherokee emerged to service the ever-increasing number of visitors.

(Top) This familiar group of characters could be seen in person at the Land of Oz park on Beech Mountain, North Carolina, from 1970 to 1980.

(Bottom) The enormous 1958 Goofy Golf course in Panama City Beach, Florida, was an eye-popping fantasyland of giant concrete figures and oversized scenery.

(Top) A popular spot for Atlanta tourists was the Wren's Nest, home of Uncle Remus creator Joel Chandler Harris.

(Bottom) Barn roofs urging tourists to "See Rock City" were among the most common sights along the Southern highways from 1936 through the 1960s.

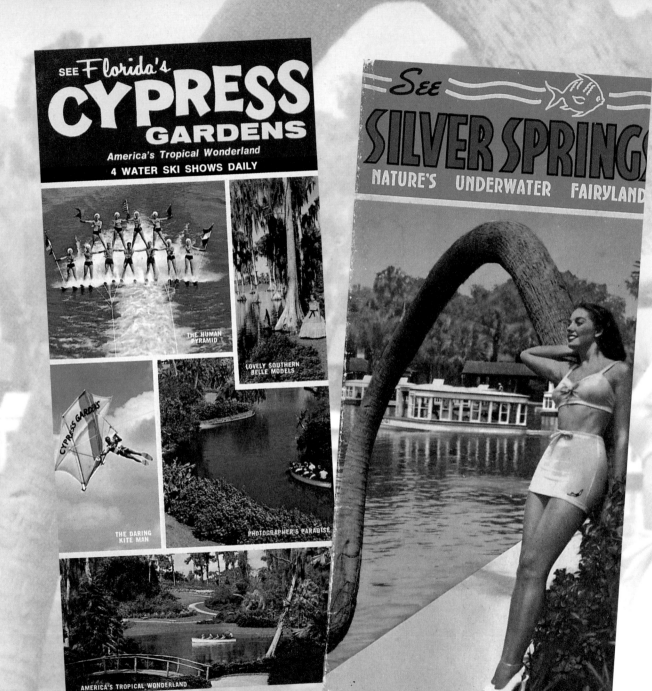

(Left) Cypress Gardens, near Winter Haven, Florida, opened in 1936, making it one of the oldest Florida attractions to still be in operation today.

(Right) Silver Springs, at Ocala, Florida, is an even older attraction than Cypress Gardens. For years it was the undisputed leader of Florida's huge tourism industry.

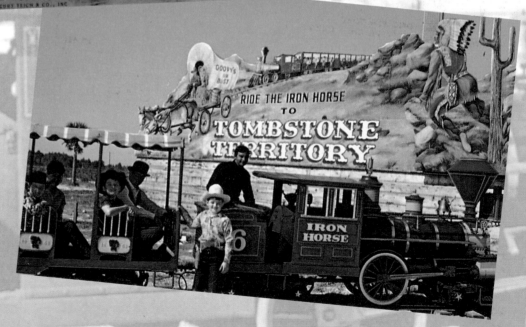

(Top) Although Silver Springs' original clientele arrived via the St. Johns River, in the early 1920s the boat traffic was halted, leaving Silver Springs as a true roadside attraction.

(Bottom) In the early 1960s, Wild West parks sprang up throughout the South due to the popularity of the TV western. Tombstone Territory in Panama City Beach, Florida, was one of several examples of this genre.

SILVER SPRINGS FLORIDA

6 Gun Territory

RIDE THE TRAIN OR SKYRIDE TO THIS TOWN OF THE OLD WEST

ADMISSION PRICE INCLUDES:

STAGE SHOW IN PALACE SALOON ★ GONDOLA SKY
STEAM TRAIN RIDE ★ THRILLING, REALISTIC GUN FIGHTS
AUTHENTIC INDIAN DANCING ★ OLD TIME "FLICKER" MOVIES

Adults $2.50 incl. tax   Children under 12 $1.25 incl. tax

CHEROKEE, N.C.
¼ mile east of Cherokee
on U.S. Highway 19

FRONTIER LAND

FORT CHEROKEE

Western Carolina's newest attraction

**INDIAN TERRITORY U.S.A.
PIONEER JUNCTION
FORT CHEROKEE**

(Left) Six Gun Territory near Ocala, Florida, was the largest and most elaborate of all the South's Wild West parks. Its site is now a shopping mall known as Six Gun Plaza.

(Right) Cherokee, North Carolina's Frontier Land was one of the last of the Wild West parks to ride into town. Its former location is now home to Cherokee's glitzy Harrah's Casino.

Brer Rabbit leads the washboard band in the Tales of the Okefenokee dark ride at Six Flags Over Georgia.

What caused the "modernization" of such formerly simple attractions as Magic World and Santa's Land? It was the advent of a new form of tourist destination: the theme park. While it is agreed that the theme park was born when Disneyland opened in Anaheim, California, in 1955, it took more than ten years for this format to reach the Southern states. When it did, it forever changed the way people thought of summer vacations.

The original attempt to bring this type of entertainment to the South ended in utter oblivion. In 1964, grandiose plans were unveiled for a 200-acre complex near Huntsville, Alabama, to be known as Space City USA. Whereas Disneyland had its own set of "lands," Space City USA was to have been divided into separate themed areas as well: Space Plaza, Moon City, Dead Man's Island (with a pirate theme), The Old South, Old Travel Town, Land of Oz (which featured plenty of other fairy tale characters as well), and the Lost World (complete with dinosaurs) were some of the elements that seemed to be derived from the appeal of already established attractions. An opening date of 1966 was announced, but in fact, and for reasons that have vanished along with it, the park never made it beyond the first stages of construction.

Space City USA never having gotten off the launching pad, it was another two years before the first Southern theme park actually opened its gates. Millionaire Angus Wynne Jr. had built the first Six Flags theme park between Dallas and Fort Worth, Texas, in 1961. Clearly and admittedly modeled after Disneyland, Six Flags Over Texas used as its theme the six different countries that had possessed the state over the centuries. Wynne's stated goal was to create theme parks that would be closer to the visitors' homes, rather than requiring long journeys to California. Six years later, he built his second such park near Atlanta. Six Flags Over Georgia opened on June 16, 1967; a day's adult admission was $3.95. (Yes, you read that correctly.) The first brochure produced for the new park read in part, "Nothing like this has

The Log Jamboree made a big splash when Six Flags Over Georgia opened in 1967.

ever been seen in the Southeast. Here is no mere amusement park. For within this 276-acre wonderland the colorful history of Georgia and the South comes alive."

Like its Texas predecessor, the original concept of Six Flags Over Georgia was that each of the park's six sections would pay tribute to a particular period in Georgia's history. Each and every ride, shop, and attraction was given some sort of historical tie-in. In the British section, the antique Hanson car ride was prefaced by the notation that the Hanson automobile had been manufactured in Atlanta from 1918 to 1924. The focal point of the Spanish section was the imposing Fort DeSoto, modeled closely on a real structure in St. Augustine, Florida. One of the park's two railroad stations was given the name of Marthasville, an early moniker of Atlanta itself. Even the locomotives themselves were scale replicas of the *Texas* and the *General,* the two trains that battled it out during the "Great Locomotive Chase" of the Civil War.

In the Confederate section, the centerpiece was the Tales of the Okefenokee dark ride, which depicted scenes from the old plantation legends made famous by Georgia author Joel Chandler Harris in his Uncle Remus stories. In fiberglass boats, visitors rode through the animated dioramas, narrowly escaping the traps set by Brer Fox and Brer Bear, and watching Brer

Rabbit outwit his adversaries at every turn. In the French section of the park could be found a similar outdoor ride illustrating some of the famous moments in the career of early Georgia explorer Jean Ribaut. This riverboat ride ended with a furious battle against the English defenders of burning Fort Argyle.

The USA, or modern section of the park, had less to do with history, but was not short on entertainment value. Famed puppeteers Sid and Marty Krofft (who had redesigned the Okefenokee ride after its first season) staged elaborate puppet shows in a specially built theatre. At the Humble Oil Company's Happy Motoring Freeway, it was Six Flags instead of Hertz who put kids in the driver's seat. The Sky Hook, a transplant from a World's Fair of years past, carried passengers aloft for an eagle's eye view of the park and the Atlanta skyline.

But times changed for Six Flags just as they did for the other Southern attractions. The public demanded newer, bigger, and faster

Six Flags Over Georgia didn't skimp when it came time to market souvenirs.

DOGPATCH USA
DOGPATCH, ARKANSAS

FIRST
CLASS
POSTAGE

Wolf Island Paddle Boats

thrill rides (or "screamers," as they became known in the trade). For years, the most exciting rides at Six Flags were the relatively tame Log Jamboree, meant to represent early Georgia's logging industry, and the rambunctious little Dahlonega Mine Train. In 1973 Six Flags began moving away from its historical angle when it presented the Great American Scream Machine, an aptly named high-speed roller coaster. From that point on, thrills, not history, would be the park's raison d'être. Six Flags drove this home when they adopted a new advertising slogan: "The Land of Screams and Dreams."

By 1976 the Kroffts had departed to open their own indoor amusement park, The World of Sid and Marty Krofft, in downtown Atlanta's new Omni complex. Their park was a resounding failure and closed within six months; its former location is now home to CNN Studios. In 1980, Tales of the Okefenokee was dismantled and replaced with the Monster Plantation, and Jean Ribaut's Adventures met the same fate the following year, becoming known as

Thunder River. The Happy Motoring Freeway had been bulldozed in 1976 for a parachute drop ride, the Great Gasp, which was simply a recycled version of an idea from the 1939 New York World's Fair. The Hanson auto ride was taken out of the British section, where it at least had some tie to reality, and placed in a more convenient spot to make room for another "screamer" attraction. Most visitors to today's Six Flags Over Georgia have no inkling that at one time it was meant to depict various eras in the history of the South. Of course, judging from the crowds that pack the parking lot every day it is open, most of them probably don't care!

Hot on Six Flags' heels, another theme park with a Southern flavor began to take shape in the Ozarks in October 1967. Dogpatch USA, as it was called, was the brainchild of a group of Harrison, Arkansas, businessmen who managed to convince Al Capp, creator of the renowned *Li'l Abner* comic strip, that the world he had developed around his newsprint characters would make an ideal attraction in the Arkansas hills. The cartoonist enthusiastically agreed, even going so far as to state that he had always thought of his fictitious Dogpatch as being in Arkansas. Everyone conveniently ignored the fact that the first *Li'l Abner* strips of 1934 specifically placed the locale as "Dogpatch, Kentucky."

Nevertheless, when Dogpatch USA opened on May 18, 1968, it attracted a lot of attention. The fact that *Li'l Abner* was at that time running in more than 1,300 newspapers, and Al Capp was a well-known (if not always liked) public speaker, made it a presold property. Once guests were transported from the parking lot to Dogpatch via a small incline railway, they could explore the world Capp had been building in the funny papers for 34 years. Li'l Abner and Daisy Mae were there, natcherly, along with Mammy and Pappy Yokum. Other characters, such as Hairless Joe, Lonesome Polecat, Moonbeam McSwine, and the rest of the motley crew, made less frequent appearances. The town square was decorated with a huge statue of the Dogpatch founder, Confederate General Jubilation T. Cornpone, who did not know the meaning of the word "fear." "Terror yes, but fear never," as the explanation went.

The world of Dogpatch itself was basically the whole attraction. There was a train ride, as pioneered by Disneyland and Six Flags, and nearby Mystic Caverns were purchased and renamed Dogpatch Caverns. Other than that, fishing and taking it easy were the main activities, much as life in the comic strip itself was depicted. As the years loped by, Dogpatch fell into the same scream-happy trap as all of the other theme parks, and such rides as Earthquake McGoon's Brain Rattler, a Space Shuttle

Li'l Abner, Daisy Mae, and Marryin' Sam pose with the statue of Dogpatch USA founder Gen. Jubilation T. Cornpone.

ride, and a Paratrooper Ride were added to the mix. But no matter what was done to increase its appeal, Dogpatch USA was founded on the popularity of the *Li'l Abner* comic strip itself, and when the strip was discontinued in 1977, and Al Capp himself died two years later, it spelled some mighty hard times for Abner, Daisy Mae, and the gang. For a while, Dogpatch was able to hang on by a thread, depending on tourists headed for Branson, Missouri, but that thread finally broke, and after its 1993 operating season Dogpatch was sent to that same heaven wherein reside the *Li'l Abner* strip and all of its charming characters. With the

H. R. Pufnstuf's sidekicks Cling and Clang serve as meeters and greeters at Six Flags Over Georgia, 1972.

park gone, at the end of 1997 the town of Dogpatch, Arkansas, also gave up and reverted to its pre-tourism name of Marble Falls.

All tourist attractions in the southeast felt the influence when Walt Disney World zip-a-dee-doo-dahed its way into Orlando in 1971, but none more so than the other theme parks. Since there were not many companies with either the financing or the creative imagination to devise attractions such as those offered by Disney, other theme parks tried to compete in the only ways they knew how. For Six Flags Over Georgia, this translated into the introduction in 1972 of costumed characters roaming the park. With Sid and Marty Krofft still in place, Six Flags' initial costumed greeters took the form of characters from the successful Krofft television programs (H. R. Pufnstuf and his friends). After the Kroffts' departure various other characters filled in.

When Opryland USA opened in Nashville, Tennessee, in 1972, it too featured larger-than-life characters, but Johnny Guitar, Delilah Dulcimer, Frankie Fiddle, and their pals just didn't have what it took to make it, and Opryland soon wisely switched over to a more appropriate adult approach. Of course, Dogpatch USA had always spotlighted its actors costumed as the comic strip characters, so it was ahead of the game in that regard. For many years Carowinds, a theme park located near Charlotte, N.C., was the home of Yogi Bear, Huckleberry Hound, Scooby Doo, and the rest of the Hanna-Barbera menagerie. Even Rock City, a longtime holdout against fads, made a concession to this trend and added costumed figures of Humpty Dumpty, Little Red Riding Hood, Mother Goose, and other residents of Fairyland Caverns.

By contrast, there was another genre of fantasy to be found along the roadside that seemed rather timeless. This took the form of giant statues that stood in front of various types of businesses, serving as lures to draw curious patrons into the parking lot. Huge roosters wearing chefs' clothes could be seen at many drive-in restaurants that served fried chicken, and fiberglass giants with sinister grins often guarded tire or auto parts dealerships. In the mountains, there were various roadside stops where children could have their photos taken with dinosaurs or Western figures...for a price, of course.

In Panama City Beach, where giant figures threatened to outnumber the tourists, an enormous pirate literally served as a building within himself. Crafted of styrofoam, with a fiberglass skin to fend off inclement weather, the bucktoothed buccaneer originally contained a wax museum of dioramas depicting pirate scenes. That enterprise failing, he was moved to the beach's Petticoat Junction amusement park, where he served as a roadside lure for a paddleboat ride over a small lagoon. After that attraction had come and gone, he sat alone, a forlorn figure, until a fire in 1993 reduced him to a pile of charred foam.

In contrast to the sad fate of the giant pirate, sometimes a figure became so famous that it turned into an attraction all its own. Such was the case of Birmingham, Alabama's 56-foot-tall cast iron statue of Vulcan, the mythological god of fire and metalworking. Standing on a 124-foot pedestal beside U.S. 31 as the highway snaked over Red Mountain, Vulcan became *the* emblem of Birmingham, even after the city's iron and steel industry had given way to other enterprises.

Vulcan had been cast as a Birmingham exhibit at the 1904 World's Fair, but after the fair was over he was returned to Alabama, where he received a less-than-hearty welcome. No one seemed to know what to do with a five-story deformed giant whose posterior was fully exposed by his leather apron, so for years he lay in rusting pieces beside the railroad tracks where he had been dumped. Finally, he was

taken to the Alabama State Fairgrounds on U.S. 11, reassembled (incorrectly), and used for all manner of tasteless advertising schemes. He was even painted to look more realistic, given a bright blue apron and flesh-colored skin, with jet black hair and eyebrows.

Someone eventually decided that the iron giant deserved better, and by 1939 the stone pedestal had been built on Red Mountain, for Vulcan to awe travelers ever after. A remodeling program in the early 1970s added an elevator shaft to the tower, and covered the beautiful natural stone with a shockingly white marble finish, but plans are now afoot to restore the park, and the old statue himself, to their original 1939 appearance.

Stories like Vulcan's are definitely the exception when it

The giant chicken beckoned to hungry travelers on U.S. 31 south of Nashville, Tennessee.

This giant pirate was a U.S. 98 landmark in Panama City Beach, Florida, for some 30 years.

Birmingham's giant statue of Vulcan, assembled incorrectly at the Alabama State Fairgrounds on U.S. 11.

comes to the fantasy-oriented type of tourist attraction. More than any of the other categories, children's attractions seem especially susceptible to change. Perhaps it is because what seemed incredible or fantastic thirty to forty years ago no longer looks relevant to today's TV-and-Disney World-weaned youngsters. For that matter, much of what the Disney parks do is simply a more high-tech version of what has gone before. In the spring of 1998 there was much hoopla when the fourth Disney theme park in Orlando opened. Known as Disney's Animal Kingdom, it featured an updated rendition of the old concrete dinosaur attractions, and was otherwise a close relative of Florida's pride of jungle-themed parks (which we will push aside the foliage and peer at in chapter 9).

Officials at Rock City have stubbornly maintained the original 1947 look of Fairyland Caverns for just such reasons, resisting suggestions that the blacklit sculptures be replaced with animatronic robots. "This is so people can see how we were entertained *before* television," they say. And they are right. Today's children may find it hard to fathom that such simplicity was once the height of excitement on any vacation trip, but as for yesterday's children, the parents and even grandparents of today, such memories are perfectly clear...and cherished.

Old Times There are Not Forgotten

Save your Confederate money, boys . . . the South will rise again!

—Popular saying in Dixie

Tourist destinations in the South were as varied as the tourists who paid to visit them. Some, such as the amusement parks along the beaches, were meant as nothing more than diversions; cotton-candy-covered cardboard cornucopias for families who wanted to get away from hum-drum, everyday life. Others, such as Rock City and Cypress Gardens, appealed to the lovers of nature and its unspoiled beauty. Then there was another class of attraction that aimed its guns (sometimes literally) at those who desired to mix a little education in with their vacations . . . frequently over the protests of their children, who would rather be riding the Great American Scream Machine at Six Flags Over Georgia. These attractions used history as their main selling point.

Inasmuch as the era of the Civil War is what most people associated with the South, it should come as no surprise that it was the historical epoch promoted most heavily in the region. In fact, the battlefields of the war were among the first locales to attract tourists in the years after the conflict. At one point, Southern historian Thomas D. Clark (who did not even try to disguise his contempt for roadside tourism) made the comment that the congestion of automobiles and the hordes of tourists flocking to the Southern battlegrounds had rendered these spots more dangerous to life and limb than they had been while the actual battles were taking place!

In most cases, the entities that ended up with control of them did a creditable job of preserving the battlefields relatively uncommercialized. Usually a small museum of some type was the only nonoriginal construction. At Point Park, site of part of the battle of Lookout Mountain, the museum displayed Civil War and Indian artifacts, but with a different type of exhibit thrown in as well. This Lookout Mountain Museum boasted life-sized dioramas

FREDERICKSBURG
VIRGINIA

depicting important events in Lookout Mountain and Chattanooga history. The figures in these dioramas were executed by the talented Jessie Sanders...yes, the selfsame sculptor responsible for the fanciful characters who populated Fairyland Caverns at Rock City!

It would be impossible to enumerate all of the battlefields that became tourist hot spots, but probably the most well known of these would be those at Richmond, Fredericksburg, and New Market, Virginia; Shiloh, Tennessee; Vicksburg, Mississippi; and the Chickamauga-Chattanooga complex along the Georgia-Tennessee border. Forts were also restored and preserved, such as the one where the whole ugly mess started, Fort Sumter in South Carolina, and two battlements, Fort Morgan and Fort Gaines, which glare at each other across Mobile Bay, Alabama. One writer has

commented that, if there is a lesson to be learned from visiting Civil War battle sites, it is that the history books are always written by the victor.

The biggest monument of all to the Confederacy, in concept as well as sheer size, would have to be Stone Mountain, on U.S. 78 near Atlanta. While the "great gray egg lying half-buried on a vast plain," as an early explorer described it, had been known to tourists for centuries (someone even erected that old tourism standby, an observation tower, on top of it in 1838), it was not until 1915 that the United Daughters of the Confederacy conceived the idea of using the vast face of the mountain for a gigantic memorial carving. The original concept for the sculpture was so impractical that it makes the mind reel: a continuous procession of Confederate officers and soldiers, both afoot and horseback, carved in the round, encircling the entire seven-mile circumference of the mountain! Since the project was scheduled to be completed sometime within the

OLD COURTHOUSE MUSEUM

VICKSBURG
MISSISSIPPI

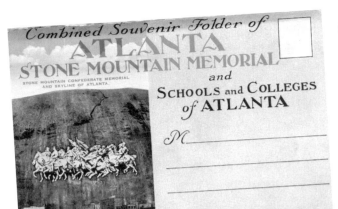

This 1920s postcard folder depicts Stone Mountain towering over the downtown Atlanta skyline, which in reality is several miles away.

Stone Mountain's massive Confederate Memorial Hall was never actually constructed, but that didn't prevent it from being pictured on the attraction's postcards.

next 1,000 years, this idea was soon whittled down to a bas-relief carving of Jefferson Davis, Robert E. Lee, and "Stonewall" Jackson, all on horseback.

A talented but temperamental artist, Gutzon Borglum, was employed to create the piece, and slowly and painfully work got underway in 1916. The family who owned the mountain set a twelve-year deadline for the project's completion, but it did not take long to see how impossible that was going to be. In 1923 the head of General Lee was unveiled, but then problems arose. Borglum had a dispute with the association that was managing the whole project, and the end result was that he took his sketches and models and went home. Let us not feel too sorry for Borglum, however. He later chiseled out his own place in history by carving Mount Rushmore.

Various methods of raising funds for the project were tried, but one of them ranks as truly unique for the tourism industry. Before Borglum left, he convinced his friend, President Calvin Coolidge, to have a special half dollar piece minted. The coins bore his version of what the carving was to look like; the idea was that they would be sold at above face value, and the resulting profits would go toward the cost of the sculpture. Reports are that this project was doomed from the start, but Stone Mountain is probably the only commercial attraction to ever be commemorated on legal United States currency!

In 1925 a new sculptor, Augustus Lukeman, was hired to complete the job, and one of his first acts was to blast away what Borglum had already finished. Beginning anew, Lukeman also got only as far as Lee's head before the 12-year deadline ran out, the family reclaimed the mountain, and it looked like the end had come. While it lasted, though, the mountain's promoters wasted no opportunity to show the public what they intended to do. Stone Mountain stands above all other attractions when it comes to the number of postcards that were issued depicting things that never actually existed. A huge Confederate Memorial Hall, to have been built *inside* the mountain's base, and at least a half dozen different versions of what the finished sculpture was supposed to look like, are among the fictionalized visions the optimistic postcard makers produced.

After sitting undisturbed for thirty years, Stone Mountain rumbled back to life in 1958. That year, the state of Georgia purchased the peak and the 3,200 acres that surrounded it, with the intention of developing it into a state park. Immediately, Stone Mountain began to take on more and more of the appearance of a real tourist attraction rather than just a carving. The Stone Mountain Scenic Railroad began operation, complete with a traditional Western cowboys-and-Indians shoot 'em up (at a Civil War park?). A typical antebellum plantation, Stone Acres, was set up to demonstrate lifestyles of the rich and Confederate, while the paddlewheel riverboat *Robert E. Lee* plied the waters of Stone Mountain Lake. (On the shore, tourists could be observed "waiting on the *Robert E. Lee*.")

Meanwhile, work on the centerpiece attraction, the sculpture itself, resumed under the direction of new artist Walker Hancock. At long last, the 90 × 190-foot carving was dedicated in 1970 and considered complete. "Consid-

ered complete" is a good term to use, because even in its final form the work depicts the three Southern heroes only from their horses' stomachs up. With its subjects' lower extremities left to the viewer's imagination, the Stone Mountain Memorial still exudes a feeling of incompleteness...an appropriate ending for its troubled history.

Another Confederate memorial with an even longer history than Stone Mountain is Atlanta's famous Cyclorama painting, even though its status as a Southern attraction was never intended at the time of its creation. Painted in 1885, it was the brainchild of one William Wehner, owner of an art studio in Milwaukee. Fifty feet in height, 400 feet in circumference, and weighing 18,000 pounds, the circular painting was meant to depict the 1864 battle of Atlanta. It was first exhibited in Detroit, Michigan, in 1887. It traveled to cities across the United States for several years after that. If people could not get

Kids could build their own cardboard replica of the Stone Mountain Park locomotive, the *General II*.

Copyright 1965
City of Atlanta, Georgia

to the South in person, at least the South, in the form of this painting, was able to come to them!

In 1892, the painting finally arrived in Georgia. The following year, it was purchased at an auction by local citizen George Gress, who in turn presented it to the city of Atlanta in 1898. The piece of art was placed in the city's Grant Park, in a less-than-imposing wooden structure. Finally, in 1921 a new marble building was constructed especially to serve as the painting's home. The addition that finally elevated the painting to its status as a major attraction came about in 1936. Through a WPA grant, the flat painting became the backdrop for an elaborate, continuous diorama of blasted tree stumps, bushes, shrubbery, broken rails and cross-ties, and plaster Confederate and Union soldiers, all enhanced by special lighting and sound effects. The total impression was overwhelming to many.

It should be mentioned that deep within the Cyclorama rests an inside joke. In December 1939, the world premiere of *Gone with the Wind* was held in At-

lanta, and most of the film's cast was on hand, touring the city and visiting the sites they had recreated for the movie. Upon visiting the Cyclorama, Clark Gable facetiously remarked that the whole thing would have been better if he had been in it. Taking the star's merry jape to heart, the artists went back to work, and today, among the hundreds of writhing figures that people the Cyclorama's foreground, there is a wounded soldier with the smiling, unmistakable face of Rhett Butler himself.

The suffix "-rama," as in "Cyclorama," really made its way into the roadside landscape after the movie process "Cinerama" was unveiled in 1952. Despite the fact that Atlanta's painting had borne that name at least since the 1920s (records are vague on that point), during the 1950s any business that wanted to show how modern and up-to-date it was would tack "-rama" on the end of its name. Suddenly the nation's highways were lined with Bowl-A-Ramas, Skate-A-Ramas, Snake-A-Ramas, and many other variations on the theme. Another Civil War attraction that fell into this linguistic pattern was the Confederama, at the base of Lookout Mountain.

In 1957, the Confederama began depicting the battles of Chattanooga, Chickamauga, and Lookout Mountain with a 480-square-foot reproduction of the local terrain. Six thousand miniature soldiers populated the Lilliputian landscape, with flashing guns and puffs of smoke, as prerecorded narration detailed the story of this decisive conflict. The recreation was the brainchild of *Chattanooga Free Press* editor Lee Anderson and his partner Pendel Meyers, both avid Civil War buffs. The Confederama was originally located in Tiftonia, Georgia, but a few years after opening the attraction moved into a new building on the Chattanooga side of Lookout Mountain, where there was heavier tourist traffic.

After some thirty years or so of continuous operation, the Confederama was beginning to look a mite outdated, even for a history-themed attraction. It was purchased by Rock City Gardens in 1994, and the new owners immediately set out to update its image. First to go was the name, which smacked of a bygone era; the attraction now became the "Battles For Chattanooga Museum." The elaborate 3-D animated landscape was retained, but the ancient electronic automation system that coordinated its movements was replaced by modern-day computerized controls. The fortlike facade was removed, and the area around the building landscaped. In May 1997, the whole shooting match was relocated for the second time in its history, to the building at Point Park that had once housed Jessie Sanders's Lookout Mountain Museum dioramas.

Besides battlefield recreations, other aspects of antebellum Southern life could be found

along the region's highways. Two locomotives, the *Texas* and the *General*, which participated in a daring raid during the war, found themselves rehashed over and over again. The *Texas*

The original *General* locomotive toured the South before becoming a Chattanooga (and, later, Georgia) tourist attraction.

was retired from service in 1907 and placed in Atlanta's Grant Park as a war relic. In 1927 the engine was moved into the newly built Cyclorama building, where its future preservation was assured. The *General*, by contrast, toured expositions throughout the country and was then brought to Chattanooga as an attraction. In 1972, the historic locomotive was returned to Kennesaw, Georgia, to be exhibited within a hundred yards of the site where it had been stolen by Union soldiers in 1862. In the meantime, a replica, the *General II*, began circling Stone Mountain in the early 1960s, while the *General III* took up residence at Six Flags Over Georgia in 1967. Old trains never die; they just keep procreating!

In the world of literature, Georgia author Joel Chandler Harris's stories of Uncle Remus and the timeless folk tales of Brer Rabbit made one of the biggest impressions on the North's vision of the region. (True, *Gone with the Wind* would eventually outshine these works, but it must be remembered that the novel's author, Margaret Mitchell, did not personally live through the Civil War. Harris did, and readers were able to pick up on his firsthand knowledge of the subject.) After Harris's death in 1908, two different Georgia attractions sprang up to pay tribute to his legacy.

In 1880, around the time his first Uncle Remus stories were becoming popular, Harris had purchased a home in the unincorporated outskirts of Atlanta. His new residence was called the "Wren's Nest" after a family of birds made themselves at home in his mailbox. In 1913, the newly formed Uncle Remus Memorial Association purchased the Wren's Nest and preserved it as a museum. The association was rechartered as the Joel Chandler Harris Memorial

Association in 1957, but the Wren's Nest remains today a valuable repository of memorabilia from Harris's career.

However, down in Eatonton, the briar patch where Harris was born and bred, other critters hopped into the fun. In 1955 the Women's Club erected a brightly painted life-sized statue of that famous trickster, Brer Rabbit, on the lawn of the county courthouse. Then, in 1963, the Uncle Remus Museum came to life, housed in a building constructed from three actual Putnam County slave cabins, promoting its own exhibits of the lives of Harris and his literary creations. Something of a rivalry eventually developed between the Wren's Nest and the Uncle Remus Museum, with each having its own legitimate claim to the late author. The Brer Rabbit statue has remained silently noncommittal.

By this time, one might be led to believe that the Civil War and its era were the only elements of history that mattered in the South. True, it was a turning point in the region's past, but it was not alone in its role in tourism. Other historic events also managed to draw in the paying customers....

There were two locales in which a city became an attraction in itself: Williamsburg, Virginia, and St. Augustine, Florida. For all their similarity in results, though, the two communities came by their respective preservation efforts quite differently. In the case of Williams-

burg, commercial possibilities initially took a back seat to serious historic preservation.

Founded in 1699, Williamsburg served as the state capital of Virginia until 1781. After that, the community went into a decline . . . and a 150-year decline can do serious damage to any burg. By the 1920s, it looked like Williamsburg's historic significance might be forgotten, but in 1926, the rector of Bruton Parish Church, Rev. W. A. R. Goodwin, decided to do something about his longtime wish to preserve the most important parts of the old city. It was certainly a revolutionary idea for a Revolutionary town, and knowing that it took a lot of current currency to accomplish this, Rev. Goodwin approached tycoon John D. Rockefeller Jr. For the rest of his lifetime, Rockefeller personally contributed all of the necessary funds for the project, now known as Colonial Williamsburg.

The "restoration" of Williamsburg consisted of demolishing several hundred buildings that had been built since colonial times and restoring

ST. AUGUSTINE FLORIDA

THE NATION'S OLDEST CITY

ST. JOHNS COUNTY, FLORIDA

close to eighty surviving original structures. The real challenge came in the actual reconstruction of sites that had been lost over time, usually utilizing the originals' excavated foundations. The first restored buildings in Colonial Williamsburg were opened to the public in 1931, and the stream of visitors grew steadily for the next forty years. There have been those who carp that Williamsburg's antiseptic appearance gives the wrong impression as to what life in the American Colonies must have been like, but John D. Rockefeller was committed to his goal. "The restoration of Williamsburg," he said, "offered an opportunity to restore a complete area and free it entirely from alien or inharmonious surroundings . . . thus it made a unique and irresistible appeal." Colonial Williamsburg helped the rest of the city pull out of its slump, and today the more modern parts of the city feature all the screaming attractions necessary

to appease youngsters and teenagers who consider Colonial Williamsburg a wonderful cure for insomnia. Elsewhere in Virginia, admirers of the Revolutionary War era could visit Monticello and Mt. Vernon, the domiciles of Early American heroes Thomas Jefferson and George Washington. These estates were preserved with so much reverence and dignity, however, that they could hardly be classified as roadside tourist attractions.

As for St. Augustine, its history was well known to many in the pre-automobile era. As we have seen in earlier chapters, during the 1880s the town became a popular spot for wealthy folks to spend the winter, in the days when it was as far south as one could go in Florida. Unlike Colonial Williamsburg, St. Augustine's tourist

S.A.73—Oldest House, St. Francis Street, St. Augustine, Fla.

Sightseeing via "Horse and Buggy"

attractions developed without one central governing force, and as a result they ended up ranging from the truly historical to the merely hysterical.

Take the Zorayda Castle, for instance. Built as a residence during St. Augustine's millionaire heyday in 1883, this replica of the Alhambra palace of Spain seemed to serve no purpose other than to look out of place. Although it was later used to house the varied collections of art authority A. S. Mussallem, Zorayda's only real connection to St. Augustine's past seems to be that both had Spanish origins. Then there were the famous Oldest House, Oldest School, and Oldest Store, the basic structures of which all dated back to the 1700s. The Old Jail went after a more sensational approach, with its graphic depictions of prison horrors and almost spookhouse-like façade. Tourists could visit the fabled Fountain of Youth, supposedly the same one "discovered" by Ponce de Leon. In the same park with the Fountain were the excavated skeletons of ancient Indians, which seemed to say something or other about the Fountain's alleged magical powers.

Another way St. Augustine's approach differed from that of Colonial Williamsburg was that not all of its area attractions even attempted to tie in with local history. The St. Augustine Alligator-Ostrich Farm was established in 1893 for the purpose of raising alligators for their

hides, and also to supply living, breathing specimens to zoos and other such exhibits. No one seems to know just how the ostriches got into the act. Potter's International Hall of Fame, opened in 1949, has long claimed the title of "first wax museum in the United States." Further research has proven that to be an error, as there was a wax museum in New York City at least ten years prior to that, but no one has come forward to dispute that Potter's was the first such attraction in Florida—probably in the whole South. Other than that distinction, there is little to differentiate Potter's from its scores of descendants in every tourist trap; as usual, personages such as Moses and Abraham could be seen rubbing wax shoulders with Will Rogers and Dwight Eisenhower.

It probably had nothing to do with Potter's opening that the very next year, 1950, saw the establishment of St. Augustine's Ripley's Believe It Or Not Museum. This was the original in what would

come to be a whole string of Ripley attractions (we have already investigated the story behind the one in Gatlinburg, Tennessee). Unlike the others, the original Ripley's in St. Augustine did not consist of wax figures representing the cartoonist's oddball discoveries. Instead, the contents of this exhibit were the oddest and most curious of all the actual objects Ripley collected during his lifetime. The method chosen to display them also differed from future Ripley Museums. The building that housed them was built in 1885 as "Castle Warden," home of one of Henry Flagler's old Standard Oil cronies. It later became a hotel, closing down only a couple of years before the Ripley people moved in. The St. Augustine location was left in its original helter-skelter form, with Ripley's relics simply interspersed with the building's own more mundane furnishings. Apparently the St. Augustine exhibit was successful, because over the next twenty years the Ripley organization opened several more locations; unlike the original,

however, future museums would be strictly organized and divided into "theme" rooms.

There were other cities that capitalized on their historic reputations, but none with the all-consuming passion of Colonial Williamsburg and St. Augustine. New Orleans was certainly historic enough, with its famous French Quarter and annual Mardi Gras celebration, but the Louisiana locality never really made any attempt to develop tacky tourist traps to take advantage of the situation. Lexington, Virginia, and Old Salem (part of Winston-Salem), North Carolina, opted for the sterilized Colonial Williamsburg approach.

Yet another genre of historic spectacle began in the early 1940s, grew in the 1950s, and became something of a tourism fad during the 1960s: the outdoor drama. The South's climate was ideally suited for these lavish amphitheater productions, and it seems that one was produced for practically any subject that had dramatic potential.

It is a matter of record that the play that started it all was *The Lost Colony,* first produced on North Carolina's Roanoke Island around 1940. Authored by Pulitzer Prize winner Paul Green, the drama told the story of the first English colony in America. Over its long run, it made itself as much a legend as the historic events it depicted, and was responsible for helping at least one promising acting career

along: for a number of years, the role of Sir Walter Raleigh was essayed by an aspiring young North Carolina actor named Andy Griffith.

Paul Green went on to create at least six other outdoor dramas of varying fame. One of his later efforts was *Cross and Sword,* presented in St. Augustine and illustrating the first two years of that city's existence. The pageant was eventually named Florida's official state play. Green also created *The Stephen Foster Story,* the biography of the famous songwriter, for performance in Bardstown, Kentucky, and *The Common Glory* for Colonial Williamsburg.

Next to Green, the region's most prolific creator of outdoor dramas was Kermit Hunter. His first big success was the 1950 premiere of *Unto These Hills* in Cherokee, North Carolina. With the authenticity of a true reservation surrounding it, *Unto These Hills*

This brochure advertised the 1950 premiere of Kermit Hunter's *Unto These Hills.*

DANIEL BOONE
PORTRAYED IN
KERMIT HUNTER'S
HORN
IN THE
WEST

June 27 thru August 23, 1969
Nightly Except Mondays

BOONE, N. C.

Just three miles off Blue Ridge Parkway

KERMIT HUNTER'S GREAT DRAMA
CHUCKY JACK

NIGHTLY
EXCEPT SUNDAY
8:15 O'CLOCK

MIDDLE
JUNE
TO
LABOR DAY

SPECIAL SHOWING
SUNDAY NIGHT
BEFORE LABOR DAY

HUNTER HILLS THEATRE
GATLINBURG, TENNESSEE

GREAT SMOKY MOUNTAINS
HISTORICAL ASSOCIATION
A TENNESSEE NON-PROFIT CORPORATION

presented "the epic clash of the red man and the white man from the arrival in Am-erica of Hernando de Soto to the tragic removal of the Cherokees to the West." Hunter par-layed the success of his play into a string of 24 other such dramas all over the United States.

In the South, Hunter's next hit was the 1951 *Horn in the West* at Boone, North Carolina. Giving the history of the southern Appalachian Mountain settlers, it starred the town's namesake, Daniel Boone him-self. Around 1956, Hunter added the third leg of his Great Smoky Moun-tains trilogy, *Chucky Jack,* performed in Gatlinburg. This epic told the story of the little-known "fourteenth colony," the State of Franklin, and the life of the first governor of Tennessee, John Sevier. (Sevier was called "Chucky Jack" by the Cherokees because of his pioneer home on the Nolichucky River.)

The dramas of Green and Hunter may have been the most numerous, but they were not the only ones that livened up summer nights in the South. In Tuscumbia, Alabama, is Ivy Green, the birthplace of famed writer Helen

Keller. This site became the location for regular performances of *The Miracle Worker,* William Gibson's award-winning biography of the great "First Lady of Courage." Harrodsburg, Kentucky, produced *The Legend of Daniel Boone,* despite the fact that some of the same material was being covered by *Horn in the West.* The Virginia mountains jumped into the fray with *The Trail of the Lonesome Pine* at Big Stone Gap.

Now, try this on for size: One of the events depicted in *Unto These Hills* was the occasion on which Cherokee chief Junaluska saved the life of General Andrew Jackson. Some fifteen years later, after Jackson became President of the United States, one of his executive actions was to order the removal of all the Cherokee from their ancestral homelands, along what became known as the infamous Trail of Tears. At that time, Chief Junaluska was heard to remark (quite understandably) that if he had known what Jackson had in mind, he would have simply killed him while they were conveniently fighting side by side, and saved his people a lot of grief.

What does that have to do with tourism, you ask? The battle at which Chief Junaluska made his perceived mistake in saving Jackson's life occurred at Horseshoe Bend, near Dadeville, Alabama. Years later, with the fighting over, a military park was established to memorialize the battle. As with most such parks, the countryside was left untouched and unsullied . . . but that did not mean that more "popular" entertainment for the tourists could not be established nearby.

On U.S. 280, the "Florida Short Route," emerged an attraction that borrowed more than a little from Chattanooga's Confederama. Yet another fortlike structure housed "The Battle of Horseshoe Bend." Yes, this was another miniature landscape (this time with a river in it), with equally miniature soldiers and Indians. Via electronics, the battle was acted out over and over again before visitors traveled on to view the actual landscape outside.

(Before leaving the subject, we should note that Andrew Jackson's palatial home, the Hermitage, remains a popular stopover for tourists near Nashville, Tennessee. Presumably Chief Junaluska's family gets in for free.)

BATTLE
OF
HORSESHOE
BEND

✱ Special School & Group Rates ✱

Become an eyewitness to history

SEE—IN AMAZING ACTION
—SOUND AND COLOR—
"THE END OF A NATION"
The Greatest War Story Ever Told—In Miniature
"OPEN ALL YEAR"
Located near Horseshoe Bend National Military

June 5, 1961

ROOSEVELT'S

LITTLE WHITE HOUSE

WARM SPRINGS, GEORGIA

The Famous "Unfinished Portrait"

VISITORS WELCOME
OPEN EVERY DAY OF THE YEAR
Hours: 9 to 5 — Weekends June, July and August: 9 to 6.

Lest we forget, not all history took place centuries ago. Attractions have also been built around more recent events, such as World War II. No, the South does not have any miniature battlefields recreating the bombing of London or anything like that, but at least a couple of ships from that conflict ended up coming home to their namesake states for a dignified honorable discharge.

The first of the pair to arrive in the South was the *U.S.S. North Carolina*. Launched in 1941, the battleship served all over the Pacific during the war, but in peacetime was considered worthless. When word got out that the mighty ship was scheduled to be scrapped, the citizens of North Carolina got together, raised $330,000 to purchase the boat, and docked it permanently along U.S. 17 in Wilmington in October 1961.

Perhaps inspired by this success, in January 1965 the 1942 *U.S.S. Alabama* was berthed alongside U.S. 90 in Mobile Bay. Both battleships attracted huge crowds and produced vast lines of souvenir merchandise. In 1969, the *Alabama* was joined in the drink by a World War II submarine, the *U.S.S. Drum*, which had no prior connection with Alabama.

Meanwhile, the president under which the two battleships had served in wartime had Southern connections, too. Franklin D. Roosevelt first visited the summer resort community of Warm Springs, Georgia, in 1924, looking for thermal waters in which he could exercise his polio-stricken limbs. He was so impressed with the results of his visit to the springs that he decided to build his own cottage there. Inasmuch as its construction was finished early in 1933, around the time of the first of his four inaugurations as President of the United States, the Roosevelt cottage was nicknamed the "Little White House."

After a Depression and 99

"Brother Joseph" Zoettl, founder of Ave Maria Grotto.

percent of World War II, Roosevelt passed away during a visit to the Little White House on April 12, 1945. On October 23, 1948, the Little White House was officially opened to the public as a memorial to the popular president, and since that time it has been faithfully preserved just as it was on the day he died there. If nothing else, the Little White House is a reminder of an era when United States presidents were held in considerably higher esteem than is considered desirable in these more cynical days.

Up to this point, one might suspect that the only parts of history that are important to anyone (especially tourists) are wars. Civil wars, world wars, Indian wars, wars for independence... didn't people *ever* stop fighting? Fortunately, among attractions with a historic theme, there are also those that celebrate the more peaceful and everyday side of the past.

For sheer peace and tranquility, everyone should take a close look at one Joseph Zoettl, a Benedictine monk at St. Bernard Abbey in Cullman, Alabama. Brother Joseph, as he was known among his peers, was in charge of the abbey's power plant, and in his spare time he took up the hobby of building miniature replicas of the world's great religious shrines. For building material, he used common items such as cement, stone, marbles, tiles, shells, rocks, chandelier prisms, and beads. His first miniatures were displayed on the monastery's recreation grounds, where the collection soon became known to the public as "Little Jerusalem," since most of the buildings were tiny versions of famous sites in the Holy Land.

When hordes of outsiders started arriving to view Brother Joseph's ever-growing collection, the abbot decided it would be prudent to move the display to a new location. An abandoned rock quarry near the monastery's administration building was landscaped and terraced, and on May 17, 1934, the newly-named Ave Maria Grotto was dedicated. To this day, however, many people still refer to the display by its original "Little Jerusalem" appellation.

This is the main sculpture for which Ave Maria Grotto was named.

These colorful billboards were once spread throughout the state of Alabama.

By the time Brother Joseph died in 1961, his Ave Maria Grotto had become world-renowned. Amazingly, out of the approximately 150 miniatures he constructed, only two were done from his own firsthand knowledge; the rest were built using postcards and photographs as the models. Individuals of all religious faiths have found Ave Maria Grotto to be an inspiration, both for the shrines it depicts and for the singleminded dedication of the man who created it.

The displays of Ave Maria Grotto represent historical events stretching back to Biblical days in the Holy Land, but just off U.S. 11 in Alabama, tourists could be transported to the remnants of an ancient civilization on *this* side of the Atlantic. It is estimated that in the years between 1200 and 1400, a great Indian nation thrived along the banks of Alabama's Warrior River. In time, a modern town grew on the same site, and in 1897 the community was named Moundville, in recognition of the many primitive Indian temple mounds that still existed within its environs.

During the 1920s, archeologists became interested in excavating and preserving the mounds, which led to the creation of Mound State Monument in 1933. This is one of those attractions that it takes a true world history buff to appreciate; those looking for cheap thrills are advised to look elsewhere. True, for many years the most sensational things to be seen at Mound State Monument were the excavated Indian skeletons, still lying in the poses in which they had been buried five centuries earlier. Such exhibitions of decayed ancestors eventually became irritating to their present-day descendants, so the boneyard collection is now out of public view. The park rules even prohibit digging into the ground for artifacts, so would-be souvenir hunters have to be content with the gift shop, a historic site in its own right that will undoubtedly be excavated by archeologists a few centuries in the future.

A subgenre of historical attractions were concerned primarily with the history of transportation in America. This was only appropriate, since it was such transportation that made their very existence possible. In Sarasota, Florida, the Cars of Yesterday Museum was one of the first of this type. Originally known as Horn's Cars of Yesterday, the name was altered to Bellm Cars of Yesterday in the 1960s. Under whatever name, it was soon joined by the Early American Museum at the entrance to Silver Springs. The promotional blurb for this museum said it all: "Those were the 'good old

days,' and you'll see why when you experience a journey into America's past. See vehicles built for the necessities of Washington's day; the ultimate in comfort designed for the carriage trade. Admire the first attempts by car builders to harness steam, electricity and gas. Marvel at the multi-cylindered power houses of the 1920s and 30s. This history of America 'on the go' is climaxed by the full scale replica of a giant space capsule."

As an added attraction to its antique vehicle entourage, the Silver Springs museum also featured an entire miniature circus that came to life at the push of a button, a collection of 300 antique dolls "from grandma's day," and a recreation of a 1910 fashion shop. Of course, the ironic thing is that the vehicles, toys, and fashions of the 1960s, when this museum operated, are today museum pieces and valuable antiques themselves!

If the proliferation of history-themed tourist attractions serves any purpose at all, it is to reinforce the oft-quoted theory that if people are unwilling to learn from history, they are doomed to repeat its mistakes. While history can be fascinating and enlightening, it also can be vaguely disturbing and unsettling. Why? Because while these attractions are reminding us how different life was in the past, they are simultaneously making us realize how different it will be in the future, and that someday the most "modern" elements of today's society will be nothing more than moldering relics in musty museums.

   Frightening, isn't it?

The Nature of Things

The kiss of the sun for pardon,
the song of the birds for mirth;
One is nearer God's heart in a garden
than anywhere else on earth.

—Dorothy Frances Gurney

We have already seen plenty of examples of the carnival atmosphere that could prevail in many of the South's tourist regions. But what if one were tired of mystery houses, wacky wax museums, miniaturized battlegrounds, Indian souvenirs made in Taiwan, and so on? Was there no place a weary tourist could visit where he or she could just walk quietly and actually *think*?

Fortunately, there were (and still are) such places. These attractions often fought off the trend toward "bigger, faster, louder" with a glinty-eyed determination . . . although a few of them have found themselves bending more and more in that direction, owing to the various visions of their changing ownership.

Of all the various types of tourist attractions, formal flower gardens probably have the most ancient ancestry. Originally a European concept, historians report that the most elaborate examples on the Continent featured complex landscaping dotted with statues of woodland animals and mythological characters. These gardens have been credited as the distant forebears of everything from miniature golf courses to Disneyland.

Once the garden idea spread its pollen to this side of the Atlantic, it changed its petals a bit. Instead of landscaping that showed off the talents of men, most stateside attempts strove for just the opposite: a "natural" look that disguised human intervention, while displaying the flora to best advantage.

Although the "flower garden" attractions were many, the three that made the most lasting impression on the Southern tourism industry were Magnolia Gardens in Charleston, South Carolina; Bellingrath Gardens near Mobile, Alabama; and Callaway Gardens at Pine Mountain, Georgia. Of the three, Magnolia Gardens was the oldest. Around 1830, Rev. John Drayton began work on his vast family estate, creating a 25-acre garden adjoining the 16 acres of the lawn itself. It is said that the old standby of all Southern gardens, the azalea, was first imported to this country by Rev. Drayton in 1843. It is impossible to separate Magnolia Gardens'

Magnolia Gardens in Charleston, South Carolina, was one of the oldest attractions of its kind in the South.

early history as a local residence from its role during the automobile tourism years, because, especially to the good citizens of Charleston, it is an institution that has seemingly always existed.

Down in Mobile, a chap by the name of Walter D. Bellingrath made his considerable fortune by founding the Coca-Cola bottling company of that city in 1903. In 1917, Bellingrath and his wife Bessie purchased a piece of property along the Isle-aux-Oies River to use as a fishing lodge. Just to dress the place up a bit, Bessie began planting (you guessed it) azaleas around the property. A trip to Europe in 1927 showed the couple what could be done with for-

mal gardens, and they returned to Mobile with an inspiration.

In 1932, Bellingrath Gardens was officially opened to the public. The response to the Bellingraths' invitation to see their display was so overwhelming that the highway patrol had to be called in to help untangle the opening day traffic snarl. The gardens were a Southern tradition by the time the Bellingraths passed away, she in 1943 and he in 1955. Like many philanthropists, before his death Bellingrath established a charitable foundation to help fund colleges and churches throughout the South. Bellingrath Gardens also remains under the control of this foundation.

A similar nonprofit organization was the force behind Georgia's Callaway Gardens, established in 1952 on U.S. 27. Their statement of purpose is simple: "Callaway Gardens was conceived and founded by Cason J. Callaway Sr. for the benefit of mankind. Its purpose is to create and maintain a place where all may find beauty, peace, inspiration, knowledge, and wholesome exercise and recreation." The same could possibly be said for nature attractions as a whole, but Callaway augmented his gardens (containing, yes, 700 varieties of azaleas) with golf courses, restaurants, a lake (complete with white sandy beach), a

Callaway Gardens

On U.S. 27 at Pine Mountain, Georgia 31822

"So Much To See and Do"

Callaway Gardens advertising from the 1960s.

This 1935 Rock City postcard features the early "See Five States" slogan.

horticultural center, a butterfly conservatory, and other such serene features. Of the three primary garden attractions, Callaway probably remains the most well-known on a nationwide basis, although more for its championship golf courses than for its flora.

While all of these gardens were lovely, it cannot be denied that for some tourists they seemed a little stuffy. There was a definite place along the roadside for attractions that preserved nature but simultaneously made it more fun. Nature abhors a vacuum, and so does the tourism industry, so it did not take long for a more entertaining breed of garden attraction to come along.

Garnet Carter was a real estate developer on Lookout Mountain near Chattanooga. He had already made and lost a fortune by inventing the game of miniature golf (as related in chapter 5), but by the time the Great Depression hit, he was casting about for other profitable business ventures. In the early 1930s, he began paying closer attention to a project his beloved wife Frieda had originally begun as a hobby. Near their home was a section of the mountain that had been known as "Rock City" since the 1800s. The gigantic stone formations on this property were truly outstanding, and Frieda Carter had gotten it into her head to create a rock garden to end all rock gardens.

Garnet surmised that his wife might have something there, and he devoted his energies to helping her with her endeavor. Pine needle pathways were laid out, winding through the giant rocks and ending at "Lover's Leap," a giant outcropping from which it was said one could see into five states. Its nickname came from a legend telling of the Indian maiden Nacoochee, who supposedly threw herself from the

precipice in despondency over the loss of her boyfriend. Because they were also fascinated with European fairy tales, the Carters imported beautiful German statues of gnomes, Little Red Riding Hood, Rip Van Winkle, and their story-book companions, and placed these colorful figures at strategic places along their meandering pathways.

Rock City Gardens made its public debut in May 1932. Business during its first three or four years was good, but not what businessman Carter was wanting. In 1936, he had another of his legendary ideas. He hired a young sign painter named Clark Byers to travel the nation's highways, painting black-and-white Rock City ads on barn roofs from Michigan to Florida, from Texas to the Atlantic seaboard. These had the desired effect, and the barns (and later, birdhouses) reading "See Rock City" were soon familiar sights to anyone driving through the South.

And what did people see when they saw Rock City? The aptly-named Fat Man's Squeeze, a narrow fissure that required wide individuals to do a little complicated maneuvering; Mushroom Rock, which looked exactly as it sounded; the Balanced Rock, which indeed was; and several other bizarrely shaped boulders. The colorful gnomes were stationed seemingly everywhere along the trail, and deep in one cavern could be seen operating their trusty moonshine still.

Rock City's barns were probably the single most common sight along the highways of the South.

Rock City Gardens is one of the very few attractions that today looks almost exactly as it did on its opening day. The pine needle path was eventually paved with flagstone, but it still follows 90 percent of its original layout. When Umbrella Rock, another formation on Lookout Mountain's north side, began advertising that *seven* states could be seen from that vantage point, Lover's Leap also upped its state count by two, and the slogan "See Seven States from Rock City" soon made Umbrella Rock into an also-ran attraction. As has been related in chapter 5, in 1947 Rock City constructed Fairyland Caverns as a way of building up its appeal to

See Beautiful

ROCK CITY

Atop Lookout Mountain • Near Chattanooga, Tenn.
OPEN EVERY DAY OF THE YEAR

Lover's Leap in Rock City

Atop Lookout Mountain → Near Interstate Highways 24, 59, and 75

CHATTANOOGA

NORTH

children, at the same time climaxing the Carters' longtime interest in the timeless tales. In the mid-1950s Rocky, a delightfully wizened gnome dressed in red and green, was designated as Rock City's trademark character, and was heavily utilized in all of the attraction's advertising and souvenirs.

Garnet Carter was often heard to remark that of all his business accomplishments, he was most proud of Rock City because it was the one thing others could not duplicate. He was right, but only to a certain point. True enough, human beings could not create rock formations in imitation of Rock City...but that did not stop them from developing other attractions centered around such already existing formations. Even on Lookout Mountain itself, a competitor calling itself "Citadel Rocks" operated for a while. Down in Vance, Alabama, the Bama Rock Gardens looked something like Rock City would have if it had been located in Cherokee, North Carolina. In the Bama Rock Gardens, the towering stone formations competed for space with relics of the Creek Indians.

Another Rock City imitator could be found on Chandler Mountain, near Steele, Alabama. In 1957, reporter Warren Musgrove was working

on a story about the area's tomato crop when he happened across the 120 acres of weird rocks. When he opened it to the public a few years later, he called it "Horse Pens 40," because some of its natural stone corrals had been used to hide livestock during the Civil War. The property also featured such oddball sights as the Elephant Rock, Groundhog Rock, and Headless Hen Rock. There was even a scenic overlook that was a dead ringer for Lover's Leap. Over the years, Horse Pens 40 went after a more hillbilly-oriented approach than its more famous predecessor. Bluegrass and crafts festivals were held there beginning in 1961, and the attraction's postcards featured a young woman who could easily have passed for Dogpatch USA's Daisy Mae. Musgrove sold his property to other owners in 1995, but Horse Pens 40 continues to round 'em up and bring 'em in to this day.

Alabama was also the home to possibly the closest Rock City imitator in the entire South. On U.S. 43, north of Hackleburg, tourists could find Dismals Wonder Gardens, another eighty acres of natural phenomena. Dismals boasted a couple of weather-carved stone Indian faces, a Pulpit Rock, its own Fat Man's Squeeze, and a Witches' Cave. The attraction's brochure elaborated: "During the warm season, the rarest phenomenon of all occurs when the dripping rocks are aglow at night with myriads of tiny

Elephant Rock at Horse Pens 40 near Ashville, Ala.

Daisy Mae, or a close cousin, hangs out at Horse Pens 40

phosphorescent worms that twinkle like the stars above. Never explained, not found elsewhere, they are called Dismalites. In three places, phantom waterfalls add to the mystery and dreamlike atmosphere: the ear responds, but not the eye." Whew!

For reasons that are quite obvious, Florida's garden attractions did not resemble Rock City in the least. The lack of mountainous terrain saw to that. However, the highest point in the central portion of the state—324 feet above sea level!—did develop its own attraction that played an important part in the garden game. At this spot near Lake Wales, Edward W. Bok established a "Mountain Lake Sanctuary," and

in the middle of this sanctuary rose the famous Singing Tower.

Dedicated by President Herbert Hoover on February 1, 1929, the Singing Tower was certainly the most elaborate and beautiful of all the observation towers before or since. Two hundred five feet tall and built of Georgia pink marble and Florida coquina stone, the tower contained a carillon that gave it its name. In front of the tower was a large pool that created a serene reflection in its still waters. As the years went by, many people began to refer to the tower by its donor's name, so tourism literature called it the Bok Tower as often as the Singing Tower.

When Bok was asked the purpose of donating his sanctuary and tower to the public, he replied with an often-quoted speech: "Simply to create symbols of pure beauty, so as to spread the influence and power of beauty, which we need so much in this country, in our cities, our communities, and our homes. Secondly, to express my appreciation and gratitude to the American people for their kindness and generosity... extended without limit." Well said, Mr. Bok.

The SINGING TOWER FLORIDA

POSTAGE 1½ c WITHOUT MESSAGE

Florida's Cypress Gardens as it appeared in 1936, its first year of operation.

Florida Cypress Gardens Winter Haven

Nearby, another Lake Wales garden bloomed around The Great Masterpiece. The titular attraction here was an elaborate mosaic rendition of Da Vinci's famous painting of the Last Supper, but the artwork practically became lost among all of the surrounding paraphernalia. Advertising promoted the Great Masterpiece's guided tours through "picturesque gardens and the 'Forest Primeval,' " Swiss cable cars that carried guests on a half-mile ride over the tree tops, glass blowers, a Western fort, live alligators, and a wildlife show. At periodic intervals, curtains would part to reveal the Great Masterpiece itself. Presumably the other activities were there for people who wanted more excitement than standing still and looking at a mosaic.

In Winter Haven, just twelve miles from the Singing Tower and Great Masterpiece, Florida's most famous garden could be found nestled along the shores of Lake Eloise. This was the brainstorm of publicity man Dick Pope.

The story goes that Pope, an Iowa native, read an article in *Good Housekeeping* magazine about a man who opened his home to the public and began charging admission. (Although not stated, Walter Bellingrath could have been the subject of that article.) At any rate, Pope and his wife Julie decided to return to their family home in Winter Haven to attempt the same thing. Their idea was to create a "botanical wonderland" out of the marshes along the edges of the lake. Work began in 1932, with the construction of canals winding through the property. On January 2, 1936, Pope's new Cypress Gardens bloomed in all its splendor.

Cypress Gardens was to central Florida what Rock City was to the southern highlands. Publicity was the name of the game, and Pope saw to it that his gardens were never far from the attention of the media. He hired young beauties to dress in antebellum hoop skirts and pose for photos in the gardens, and installed highly-promoted "quiet electric boats" to take visitors on gentle cruises through the canals he had built. Newsreels showing Cypress Gardens' wonders were produced, and photos were distributed to every possible outlet.

One of those photos showed some youthful water-skiing enthusiasts being pulled behind a speeding boat on the lake. When this photo ran in a local newspaper in 1943, it produced an unexpected reaction. Some soldiers who were stationed nearby showed up at Cypress Gardens' gate, wanting to see the water show. That would have been ginger peachy with a cherry on top, except that there *was* no water show at Cypress Gardens. With World War II in full fury, Dick Pope was overseas, and the gardens were under the care of his wife Julie; now it was her turn to have a brainstorm. Rounding up her children and several of their friends, she quickly had them out on Lake Eloise performing whatever waterlogged stunts they could create on the spur of the moment. Word of the aquatic activities got around, and the very next weekend, 800 soldiers showed up. (One suspects that the lonely and sequestered servicemen were as anxious to see the girls in their swimsuits as they were the stunts they were performing.)

As almost everyone knows by now, water-skiing performances soon became the all-time trademark of Cypress Gardens. A commercial line of water-ski equipment was even marketed bearing the attraction's name. It is not recorded what Dick Pope thought when he returned from the war and found out about the attraction that had been added during his absence, but it is safe to assume that he was delighted at this opportunity for more publicity.

One of Pope's biggest coups in the postwar

A 1952 view of Cypress Gardens' renowned water ski show.

that movie, Van Johnson was cast as the gardens' fictitious anything-goes publicity agent, a role that may have been patterned after Dick Pope himself. Esther Williams later broadcast some TV specials from the gardens, beginning in 1960, and for one of these a special swimming pool shaped like the state of Florida was built for her use. The Aquarama pool, as it was known, remains at Cypress Gardens today. The attraction was camouflaged as extreme southern Florida for *Moon over Miami* (1941), with Betty Grable and Don Ameche, and *A Hole in the Head* (1959), with Frank Sinatra. *This Is Cinerama* (1953), the introduction to the ill-fated movie format, also included Cypress Gardens in its footage. The gardens eventually served as the backdrop for the weekly religious TV broadcast *Day of Discovery.*

Like most attractions, Cypress Gardens found itself somewhat overshadowed by the arrival of Walt Disney World . . . especially since Mickey, Donald, and friends had set up their residency right in its own backwater. Dick Pope continued to oversee operations until his retirement in the early 1980s, at which time his son Dick Jr. (one of the original waterskiers) took over. In 1985, Cypress Gardens was sold to publisher Harcourt Brace Jovanovich, who turned around and sold it to Anheuser-Busch (who already had their own gardens in Tampa) in 1989. In 1995,

years was his success in getting motion picture companies to film productions at Cypress Gardens. The attraction's list of short subject and television appearances is a long one, but in the realm of feature films, no doubt the biggest star to shine at the gardens was sensational swimmer Esther Williams. She cavorted around the property in at least two MGM musical extravaganzas, *On an Island with You* (1948), which also featured Ricardo Montalban and Jimmy Durante, and *Easy to Love* (1953), which actually weaved its entire plot around Cypress Gardens itself and the famous water-ski show. In the gardens were again sold, this time to a management group. During the tenure of its several most recent owners, Cypress Gardens has begun inching more and more toward an amusement park look, even promoting itself as "Florida's oldest theme park." Unlike Rock City, which prides itself on its deliberate lack of change, Cypress Gardens' story is more typical of older attractions' efforts to survive in a changing tourism market.

Another major class of nature attractions involves those developed around some preexisting natural feature, rather than human-made gardens and trails. One of the oldest, both geographically and historically, could be found along U.S. 11 in Virginia. Natural Bridge, as its name indicates, is a giant rock formation that was once touted as "higher than Niagara and old as the dawn." Its history as a tourist attraction stretches back to pre-Revolutionary War days, when the property was mapped out by a young surveyor named George Washington. Present-day visitors are often surprised to find his initials carved into Natural Bridge's southeastern wall. (If an attraction must be worried with graffiti, that is probably the best kind to have!) The property was purchased by one Thomas Jefferson in 1774, who went on record as stating, "Natural Bridge will yet be a famous place that will draw the attention of the world." It is interesting to note that Jefferson himself

constructed a log cabin on the site, with a room set aside for visitors . . . does this make Thomas Jefferson the first Southerner to operate his own roadside attraction?

A century passed, the age of the automobile got underway, and by the 1930s it was necessary to build the Natural Bridge Hotel to replace Jefferson's log cabin. As with most nature attractions, the various owners of Natural Bridge kept adding more and more features to complement the centerpiece. One that began more than six decades ago and is still going strong is the nightly "Drama of Creation."

A circa 1939 brochure described the pageant this way: "Here in Nature's cathedral the exalting drama of Creation is reenacted each evening. When darkness comes, symphonic music fills these ancient walls. Full-throated voices lift their soft melody, and the swell of a mighty organ drifts out upon the night. Colored lights spread a canopy of soft hues across the great stone arch, while a voice from far overhead tells the Biblical story of the dawn of the world. It is a pageant profound

Esther Williams's Florida-shaped swimming pool at Cypress Gardens.

As you can see, Virginia was not the only state to have a bridgelike rock formation.

and breathtaking, one you will never forget." It must be admitted that for a presentation of the creation of the world, it would be difficult to find a star performer closer to the proper age than Natural Bridge.

As was mentioned earlier in the discussion of Rock City, Natural Bridge was an outstanding sight to see, but not a unique one. The forces of wind and water carved out bridgelike structures in several locations. Alabama had two of them within just a few miles of each other. Rock Bridge Canyon, just off U.S. 43 near Hodges, boasted all the usual sights such as Echo Rock, Turtle Rock, Noah's Ark, and other formations. Natural Bridge of Alabama (so named to avoid confusion with the one in Virginia), near U.S. 78, was left basically as nature created it: "Only paths and picnic tables have been added for your convenience," their brochure said. Oh yeah, and also a concession building with restrooms and (surprise!) a souvenir shop.

One of the few waterfall attractions in the South could be found near Gadsden, Alabama, where Noccalula Falls Park was developed during the 1950s. Shades of Rock City's Lover's Leap, the tale was told that Indian princess Noccalula threw herself over the falls to prevent her marriage to an undesirable brave. (Didn't those Indian princesses *ever* find a way to deal with their problems other than by jumping off cliffs?) The park named in her honor featured a restored pioneer homestead and nature trails, but being under the control of the state, did not produce as many of the "tacky" Indian images as one might expect from its namesake. A bronze statue of the unfortunate Noccalula, posed on the ledge overlooking the falls, was about as creative as the park dared to be.

A rather unusual attraction grew up on the rim of Little River Canyon, a deep gorge (the deepest east of the Mississippi River, according to publicity) on the southern end of Lookout Mountain. Canyon Land Park, as the property was called, opened in 1970. Complete with its own amusement park and restaurant, the main feature at Canyon Land Park was the only chairlift in Alabama, which carried visitors deep into the bottom of the canyon itself. Unfortunately, by the time this park came along, the face of tourism was changing, and Canyon Land Park was just not visionary enough to ensure its own survival. It had closed and its rides had been auctioned off before the decade was over.

Perhaps the largest and most noticeable natural feature in the South (aside from the mountains) is the impenetrable Okefenokee Swamp on the Georgia-Florida border. Inasmuch as some of the South's earliest settlers came into Georgia by way of Florida, it did not take long

for them to discover this junglelike mass of vegetation and wildlife. The only problem was that no one knew what to call it. The native Indian population had their own word for it, a word that meant "Land of the Trembling Earth." However, since the Indians of that day had no written language, it was anyone's guess how to spell it. One historian documented at least 77 different spellings of "Okefenokee" that were used between 1776 and 1921; incredibly, these were 77 different attempts to duplicate the same sound pattern. A typical early version of the name appears on a 1763 map of Florida, which sets aside one area designated as "The Great Swamp, Owaquaphenogaw."

However it was spelled, the marsh was the property of the state of Georgia until 1890, when an Atlanta lawyer devised an elaborate scheme to drain it and leave millions of dollars worth of timber and fertile land. The plan was a failure, but it seems to have alerted authorities to the need for preserving the swamp in its natural, almost prehistoric form. In 1936 the Okefenokee National Wildlife Refuge was established, and less than ten years later Okefenokee Swamp Park set up shop with its entrance on U.S. 1, just south of Waycross, Georgia.

As is fitting, the park did not try to improve on the natural beauty of the swamp, but it did construct a museum and interpretive center to help tourists understand the mysteries of the Okefenokee. The swamp received its biggest national boost in 1949, when cartoonist Walt Kelly chose it as the setting for his wildly popular comic strip satire *Pogo*. The adventures of Pogo Possum and his animal peers brought the Okefenokee name to public attention like never before. Kelly showed his appreciation to the Okefenokee Swamp by contributing funds to the construction of the visitors' center, and the town of Waycross still pays tribute to the merry marsupial in a much-publicized festival each fall.

The last major category of nature's wonders are the caverns that were developed for human entertainment. Since one cave looks very much like every other cave, each of the attractions was faced with the daunting prospect of coming up with a selling point or a new twist to distinguish itself from all the others. This was not always successful. However, let us take a look at these underground projects, one state at a time:

Probably the most famous of all the Southern caverns is Kentucky's Mammoth Cave. Discovered in the late 1700s, Mammoth Cave has continued to live up to its gargantuan name. More than 150 miles of caverns have been explored and documented in the complex, but no one knows just how much more of it exists. Its significance is such that Mammoth Cave was designated a national park in 1936, but even before that honor, its reputation was causing an incredible amount of activity in its region of the state.

Central Kentucky's "Cave Country," as it is still known today, boasted many more crevices smaller than Mammoth, each vying for its spot in the traveler's wallet. According to some sources, by the early 1920s seventeen caves were competing with each other within this specific area. There were Diamond Caverns, Jesse James Cave, and Crystal Onyx Cave, among others, and even two cities named Horse Cave and Cave City. As we saw in chapter 2, this tourist-crazy part of Kentucky also gave birth to the undeniably eccentric chain of Wigwam Village motels.

Running a close second to Mammoth Cave in fame was Virginia's Luray Caverns. This famous cave was discovered by Andrew & William Campbell and Benton Stebbins, and the attraction's official history tells it well: "On an August afternoon in 1878, while exploring the hill, these men discovered a crevice through which cold air was escaping. After opening a large fissure, Andrew was lowered by rope into the mysterious darkness below. And there, by candlelight, he gazed in awe upon what is now known as the most beautiful cave in the world."

Luray Caverns says that it has been open to the public ever since that day, but that is not to say that improvements were not made over the next hundred years or so. One of Luray's proudest advertising points was the fact that the illumination inside was all *white* light, not the colored bulbs that most caves used for dramatic effect. A truly unique feature of Luray was its stalactite organ, an instrument that used the natural formations of the cave instead of the usual organ pipes. Up on the earth's surface, in the tradition pioneered by Silver Springs' Carriage Cavalcade and other such exhibits, Luray Caverns rolled out its Car and Carriage Caravan in the 1950s.

Virginia being one of the most mountainous of states, it is not surprising that it also held the greatest number of developed caverns. Besides Luray, travelers on U.S. 11 could visit Dixie Caverns near Roanoke and Endless Caverns near New Market. (Tourist: "Guide, how long do we keep walking in these caverns?" Guide: "Oh, we never stop . . . these are Endless Caverns!!") There were Grand Caverns at Grottoes and Skyline Caverns at Front Royal; and

"Ball Room"
THE MOST BEAUTIFUL CAVE IN THE WORLD

RUBY FALLS, 145 FT.
1000 FT. BELOW SURFACE
WORLD'S GREATEST CAVE SCE...
LOOKOUT MOUNTAIN CAVE, CHAT...

Shenandoah Caverns, in the valley of the same name, advertised with a red-and-green elf mascot who resembled a cousin of Rock City's Rocky the Gnome.

Tennessee had its share of subterranean thrills, too. One of the most beloved and most heavily advertised was discovered deep inside Lookout Mountain in 1923. Leo Lambert had devised a plan to commercialize a giant cavern at the base of the mountain that had been used as a hideout during the Civil War. Choosing a spot on the side of Lookout, Lambert began excavating an elevator shaft. However, about halfway down, the workmen unexpectedly broke through into another cavern. Exploring the passageway (largely on his stomach), Lambert found that this "new" cavern contained a spectacular underground waterfall, which he promptly named after his wife Ruby. The lower cave opened as an attraction in December 1929, followed by the public debut of Ruby Falls six months later.

On U.S. 11 (an excellent highway for cave lovers) near Sweetwater, the underground lake known as the Lost Sea had been documented as far back as 1905, but sixty years passed before it was made accessible to the public. U.S. 41 at Monteagle brought us Wonder Cave, while Crystal Cave advertised itself as "Chattanooga's Outstanding Attraction Or Your Money Back." Cudjo's Cave, whose history as an attraction dated to the pre-auto era, was nestled along the Tennessee-Virginia-Kentucky border. Bristol Caverns opened to the public in 1944, a period that was generally not so good for debuting tourist attractions. Two caves beckoned to tourists who were immersed in the wonders of Gatlinburg and the Great Smokies: Tuckaleechee Caverns debuted in 1953, while Forbidden Caverns, opened in June 1967, went after an eerie air of foreboding based on its place in Indian legend. With atmospheric lighting and stereophonic sound, Forbidden Caverns treated spelunkers to such cheery locales as the Grotto of the Dead, Ledge of the Gargoyle, and Grotto of the Evil Spirits.

One of Alabama's most notable contributions to cave lore was Sequoyah Caverns, inside Sand Mountain on cave-loving old U.S. 11. An interesting sidelight about Sequoyah Caverns is that its developer was Clark Byers, the "barnyard

Rembrandt" who had painted Rock City's barn-roof ads for thirty years. In fact, at the time Sequoyah was opened to the public, Byers was still hard at work for Rock City, so he took the opportunity to sprinkle a few inside jokes around his own attraction. Acknowledging the many roofs he had painted that advertised Rock City as "World's Eighth Wonder," his billboards for Sequoyah Caverns designated them the "World's *Ninth* Wonder." And deep in the caverns, an unlighted passageway was marked with an arrow pointing into the inky blackness. The wording on the arrow? "35 Miles to Rock City."

Near Grant, Alabama, Cathedral Caverns was credited with having the largest opening of any cave in the world. Although Cathedral remained a popular attraction for some three decades, it eventually closed in 1986 and was later purchased for possible redevelopment as a state park. The state had already purchased Rickwood Caverns near Blount Springs, but during its days as a private enterprise, Rickwood had made its own reputation as one of the busiest highway advertisers in Alabama. Its red-and-white billboards once blanketed Alabama's primary, secondary, and barely-even-there roadways. Russell Cave, near Bridgeport, generally avoided such publicity stunts, especially after it was designated a National Monument in 1961. DeSoto Caverns, near Childersburg, inherited Rickwood's mantle as

the king of roadside billboards in Alabama. Supposedly discovered by the famous explorer whose name it bears, DeSoto Caverns advertised

Tour passes "Big Rock Candy Mountain

"To the north of Snake Back Mountain,
To the east of Rocky River,
Lies a place that is Forbidden,
Hollow Mountain of Two Streams"

From an Ancient Cherokee Legend

One of Rock City barn painter Clark Byers's advertisements for his own attraction, Sequoyah Caverns on U.S. 11.

with possibly the most absurd costumed mascot in the entire industry, a cartoony Spanish conquistador dubbed "Happy Hernando." (Yes, they really did.)

The rest of the South had caves scattered here and there, but no other great concentrations of them. Arkansas' Ozark region had Crystal River Cave near Cave City and Wonder Cave at Bella Vista. For several years Dogpatch USA renamed nearby Mystic Caverns "Dogpatch Caverns," and made them into the locale where Lonesome Polecat and Hairless Joe brewed their potent Kickapoo Joy Juice. After Dogpatch was past its prime, Mystic Caverns reverted to their original name. Due to geographic features, caves were probably the one type of attraction Florida was not able to capitalize upon to any great extent, but Florida Caverns, near Marianna, did at least make an effort to fill that void.

Nature attractions like those discussed here occupy their own unique position in roadside history. They generally go after a more sophisticated and mature audience than other types, although in special cases there have been attempts to make them more interesting to the younger fun-loving set. Unlike commercial developments, which are sometimes aimed at the lowest common denominator, natural attractions continue to remind the public that the most amazing sights to be seen on earth are those not created by the hand of man.

DeSoto Caverns' "Happy Hernando" was perhaps the silliest costumed mascot in Southern tourism.

Spring Training

The glass bottom boat, you will agree,
Will show you the magic of the deep blue sea.

—Joe Lubin, "The Glass Bottom Boat"

Most of the standard tourism genres—amusement parks, observation towers, wax museums—were spread throughout any area with a heavy tourist concentration. To even the most casual observer, it would be obvious that if a particular type of attraction existed anywhere, it could probably be found in Florida as well. However, there was one realm which Florida had totally to itself, without any competition at all.

None of the other Southern states could boast of the variety of springs that could be found in Florida. Moreover, the major springs were developed as attractions that, in the pre-theme park era at least, completely overshadowed anything their lesser roadside companions might have to offer. Inasmuch as these springs were indeed unique to Florida, they deserve a closer look (perhaps even through a glass bottom boat?).

For decades, the absolute no-question-about-it king of *all* Southern attractions was Florida's Silver Springs. Even though it is still a popular spot today, there is really no way to convey just how this enterprise once dominated the whole state's tourist industry. That was due in part to the fact that it had been drawing visitors since before Florida even *had* a tourist industry.

Silver Springs was well known to the ancient Indians in that part of the state, who considered it a sacred spot in their tribal religions. Palefaces did not discover its wonders until the 1850s, and during the heyday of the Florida millionaires, Silver Springs first began to emerge as a true vacation destination. The first tourists came by steamboat, leaving from Jacksonville or St. Augustine and traveling inland via the St. Johns River.

The story of Silver Springs' big splash is connected with one Hullam Jones. In 1878, Jones affixed a glass viewing box onto the flat bottom of a conventional dugout canoe. Ostensibly, this was first done to enable workmen to locate cypress logs that lay at the bottom of the springs, but Jones's invention would soon prove to have more far-reaching influence than that. Suddenly the glass bottom boat was a reality, and when word of this window to the underwater world got out, there was no holding the people back. Records show that Silver

Springs' visitors during the 1880s and 1890s included Ulysses S. Grant and General William Tecumseh Sherman (who no doubt had to watch their backs at all times while visiting the South), Mr. and Mrs. Thomas Edison, poet Sidney Lanier, and writer Harriet Beecher Stowe.

For all its popularity among the socially prominent, Silver Springs did not become a stop for the common highway tourist until 1924, when the property was leased by a couple of Ocala businessmen, W. C. Ray and W. M. "Shorty" Davidson. This pair set out to promote Silver Springs in a big way, and one of their first acts was to halt the traffic coming in on the river, officially making Silver Springs a true roadside attraction. They got the springs designated a Registered National Landmark, and replaced the old rowboat-style glass bottom boats with a gasoline-operated variety in 1925.

Ray and Davidson also began adding other features. A noted herpetologist named Ross Allen set up his famous Silver Springs Reptile Institute during the early 1930s, shocking young and old alike with his demonstrations of "milking" the venom from rattlesnakes and other such creepy crawlies. Allen made quite a name for himself with his reptilian ramblings, and his appearances on such nationally-broadcast radio shows as *Ripley's Believe-It-Or-Not, Hobby Lobby,*

and *We The People* certainly did their part to promote Silver Springs.

During the same period, a concessionaire known as Colonel Tooey began Silver Springs' Jungle Cruise boat ride. The attraction reports: "Tooey established the first troop of wild rhesus monkeys on an island in the Silver River to attract visitors to his ride. He did not realize that rhesus monkeys are excellent swimmers. They quickly escaped, forming wild troops along the river." The Jungle Cruise, populated by descendants of Tooey's primates, is still a major part of Silver Springs.

This "jungle" attracted the attention of Hollywood filmmakers, and between 1932 and 1942 motion picture production at Silver Springs became almost a second industry. Probably the most famous features to be produced there were sequences of six MGM "Tarzan" movies starring Johnny Weissmuller, for which Silver Springs made a passable impersonation of Africa. Other productions included *Moon over Miami* (1941), which also featured footage of Cypress Gardens, and *The Yearling* (1946).

Silver Springs' burgeoning fortunes proved to be beneficial to the surrounding neighborhood.

Johnny "Tarzan" Weissmuller gets acquainted with one of his co-stars while filming at Silver Springs.

The Tommy Bartlett Deer Ranch was one of the first "extra" attractions to hook itself to Silver Springs.

A 1947 brochure gave the following update on the condition of the area's accommodations: "You have your choice of five hotel or cabin courts. None are operated by or are under the control of Ray and Davidson, but all are recommended. None is equipped for housekeeping. All are within walking distance of the springs, either down the main highway or along trails through the forest." But the attraction's relationship with the local motels was sometimes a tense one, as the same brochure pointed out. "Although hotel or cabin courts near Silver Springs invite you to stay through any season," it read, "you should understand that Silver Springs and its indescribable underwater life can be seen and enjoyed in a minimum of 90 minutes; that all of its many and varied wonders can be covered in a maximum of four hours." The brochure goes on to point out that "Silver Springs is primarily a scenic wonder to be seen between trains or buses stopping in nearby Ocala, or in your automobile while en route into or out of Florida, or as a one day or weekend objective after you have reached your Florida destination and have settled down for the season." (This last statement reflects the days when weekend trips to the Sunshine State were still in the future, and most people who visited Florida did so for a large chunk of the winter months.)

Through the 1950s and 1960s, Silver Springs continued its meteoric rise in the tourism industry. Attendance had jumped to more than 800,000 annually by 1950. Between 1957 and 1961, the successful syndicated TV series *Sea Hunt* was filmed at Silver Springs. The series' producer was Ivan Tors, who was, as we saw way back in chapter 3, quite keen on Florida location filming. The show starred Lloyd Bridges as an undersea adventurer, and the well-known clarity of Silver Springs' water was a great liquid asset.

Another showbiz personality who had made himself at home in the park by 1955 was Tommy Bartlett, well known at the time for hosting the CBS radio and television series *Welcome Travelers*. His contribution to Silver Springs was Tommy Bartlett's International Deer Ranch, where adults and children alike could get up close and personal with the relatives of Bambi and Rudolph. Perhaps because of its emphasis on deer, Bartlett's ranch employed a rather heavy Christmas theme, with the transportation wagons disguised as Santa's sleigh. It even featured its own candy-striped "South Pole."

Silver Springs had its first ownership change in forty years when the longstanding partnership of Ray and Davidson sold the property to none other than the American Broadcasting Company (ABC) in 1962. One of ABC's first changes was to remove Tommy Bartlett's name

The Toonerville Trolley transported tourists back in time at Silver Springs' Carriage Cavalcade.

gin incorporating jokes about it into their routines. Silver Springs received free advertising from rural comic Bob Corley, who built one of his monologues around a visit to the spot: "We rode out over th' clearest water, while th' boat driver named off all th' springs. They all had purty names, like th' Fairy Castul, an' th' Bridal Chamber...all 'cept one, an' hit wuz called the Bottomless Pit. Th' boat driver said, 'Friends, yo're lookin' inta th' Bottomless Pit, a spring so deep no human eye kin see to th' bottom.' Hit sorta upset me when he said that, 'cause I was a-lookin' clean to th' bottom at th' time! An' you know whut wuz down ther? Hit wuz a sign that said 'See Rock City'!"

Near Tallahassee, Wakulla Springs took several of Silver Springs' concepts and executed them in a more low-key manner. Yes, Wakulla had its own fleet of glass bottom boats, and bragged on the clarity of its waters. Wakulla even encouraged deep swimming experts by installing a "Free Air Station" 24 feet beneath the surface, for the benefit of those who found themselves out of breath at that depth. Wakulla never became quite as well-known as the springs in the central Florida region;

from the deer ranch, inasmuch as he worked for a competing network. Other features were added: the Prince of Peace Memorial housed thirteen carved scenes from the life of Christ (sort of a cross between Ave Maria Grotto and Christus Gardens, which was fairly new at the time). The Early American Museum, mentioned in chapter 6, displayed an impressive collection of antique cars, replacing an earlier attraction known as the Carriage Cavalcade. Whereas the Bartlett Deer Ranch used replicas of Santa Claus's jitney for the visitors' transportation, Carriage Cavalcade reached back into comic strip history to recreate the famous Toonerville Trolley of funny paper fame.

A tourist attraction knows it has entered the realm of popular culture when comedians be-

This 1938 postcard was one of the first items issued for the developing Rainbow Springs attraction.

Rainbow Lodge as seen in 1949.

perhaps this had something to do with the fact that there were really no other attractions in its immediate vicinity, so it could not depend on a heavy flow of already-available visitors. At any rate, Wakulla eventually left the world of commercial attractions and became a Florida state park, which it remains today.

After Silver Springs' initial rise to fame between 1924 and 1934, it took some time for others to jump into the pool. It is sometimes difficult to determine the fine line between public awareness of a natural spot and its actual development for tourists, but it seems that the next competitor to arise in Silver Springs' neighborhood was Rainbow Springs, on U.S. 41 near Dunnellon. The fact that this attraction was out of business for several years makes it even more complicated to track down its history, but it was issuing postcards at least by 1938. One of those early cards describes what was, at that time, the primary feature: "A beautiful scenic waterfall in an unforgettable tropical setting. . . . To have missed Rainbow Springs and Rainbow Falls is to

have missed the indescribable glory of tropical Florida." Apparently the waterfall was not enough, because Rainbow Springs had soon debuted a line of (surprise!) glass bottom boats. Eventually, though, the springs' primary traffic on the Rainbow River became its submarine boats, which seated passengers underwater and enabled them to see the wonders out of the portholes at eye level.

In the early 1950s, Rainbow Springs was leased by another leader in the South's tourist industry, Rock City Gardens. Rock City brought in the services of its own advertising agency, and soon barn roofs along U.S. 41 through Georgia and Florida were bearing suspiciously familiar-looking "See Rainbow Springs" signs. Around

the same time, Rainbow issued a 78-rpm record that preserved for posterity a portion of the spiels their boatmen used while cruising visitors up and down the river. An announcer gave a plug for the attraction:

Here at Rainbow Springs, we have endeavored to preserve the natural scenic beauty which surrounds the springs, and the amazing underwater creations of the Maker. Noticeably absent are the ballyhoo and commercial atmosphere which today marks many of America's outstanding attractions. In place of these, Rainbow Springs offers a quiet, restful atmosphere, timed to the carefree pace of the true Southland.

Rock City's lease on Rainbow expired in the early 1960s, and the property next became jointly owned by Holiday Inn and S&H Green Stamps. Under their control, the next ten years saw the attraction develop into exactly what the old promotional record had said it was not. It never installed a flashing neon sign to pull in drivers off U.S. 41, but more features were added that would later prove to be a mistake. One of the biggest flops was the expensive and highly promoted Forest Flite, an airborne monorail system with cars shaped like giant leaves, which whisked tourists through Rainbow Springs' jungles. Its usage, or the lack thereof, soon showed that skyrides and monorails were not the reason people came to see Rainbow Springs.

Other features that contributed to Rainbow's

decline included the unavoidable fact of its location on an old federal highway that was bypassed by I-75. It took nearly twenty minutes to drive from the interstate to Rainbow Springs, and not many people were willing to take time out to do that. Still smarting from bad financial investments such as Forest Flite, Rainbow Springs closed in early 1974, with plans in the offing to use the property as a housing development. It appeared that Rainbow Springs was going to be one attraction that had no pot of gold at its end. However, the state of Florida jumped in with both feet and purchased the property from its would-be developers. After more than twenty years, Rainbow Springs State Park finally reopened in March 1995, preserving the attraction's colorful history, but minus the commercial hoopla of Rainbow Springs' last years.

The other Florida springs did not join the fun until the postwar era. In fact, the war was directly responsible for one of them. In 1946, ex-Navy frogman Newton Perry purchased a spring at the head of the Weeki Wachee River. Looking about for a way to capitalize on his investment, Perry reached into his own military background for inspiration. His brainstorm was that young ladies could learn to perform acrobatic stunts *under water,* all the while replenishing their lungs with compressed air being

Weekiwachee Springs, Florida On U.S. 19 - Sharing Air Hose 50 ft. Below The Surface As Seen From The Underwater Theatre. Gegerberg Photo

This postcard indicates that in the early days, Weeki Wachee's underwater shows featured both male and female performers.

but either "winding spring" or "little river.") Originally, viewers on the dry side of the windows merely saw the spectacle of girls in swimsuits reenacting ballet poses underwater. When the novelty of this wore off, the "mermaids" began elaborate productions that were usually based upon familiar stories. *Peter Pan, Alice In Wonderland, The Wizard of Oz,* and other such classics were all eventually subjected to soggy adaptation.

The stunts of the Weeki Wachee Mermaids were truly amazing. Only one year after the attraction's opening, it was being used for underwater sequences in the Universal picture *Mr. Peabody and the Mermaid,* starring William Powell, even receiving recognition by name in the film's opening credits. Mermaids became the absolute trademark of Weeki Wachee, even though the swimmers performed in bathing suits more often than in their fake fish tails. Graceful white mermaid statues lined the spring's entranceway, while the Mermaid Motel opened for business directly across the street. Just as the sailors of legend had discovered, at Weeki Wachee it was impossible to escape from the mermaids' clutches.

In 1959, Weeki Wachee was purchased by the ABC network, who would also acquire Silver Springs a few years later. Once the two attractions came under the same ownership, much mutual promotion ensued. On June 6, 1973,

fed through hoses. Perry built a theater to showcase his sopping new performers; the audience was seated fifteen feet below the water's surface, and viewed the show through gigantic plate glass windows that looked out onto the alien submarine landscape of the spring.

The first "live underwater mermaid show" was presented to the public on October 13, 1947, and the new Weeki Wachee Spring was launched. (Actually, in the earliest days, "Weekiwachee" was spelled as one word. Its origin was an Indian phrase meaning not "ladies who swim while wearing zip-on fish tails," as one might suspect,

ABC even broadcast a musical special, *The Wacky Weeki Wachee & Silver Springs Singing & Comedy Thing,* starring actor Tony Randall, which amounted to a long, long commercial for both attractions. (Although Silver Springs and Weeki Wachee were eventually sold off by ABC, they remain under common ownership today.) Also during the ABC years, Weeki Wachee's promotional literature featured a record number of celebrities: Roy Rogers, rocket scientist Werhner Von Braun, radio personality Don McNeil, Don Knotts, Bob Hope, Arthur Godfrey, and others... all endorsing the mermaid show. Weeki Wachee was the site of the 1964 premiere of Don Knotts's movie *The Incredible Mr. Limpet*...somewhat unusually, since in that particular film all of the underwater sequences were actually animated cartoons.

Most of the standard features could be found supplementing the main show at Weeki Wachee. There were glass bottom boat rides (hardly surprising by this time) and a jungle cruise with live animals. A more unusual item was the Wilderness Train, a tram-style vehicle that ran through the Florida jungle and offered a stop at "Florida's only authentic Seminole Indian ghost village." This recreation of an abandoned Indian camp at least saved Weeki Wachee the expense of hiring actors to play the parts of the Indians.

The last of the springs to become an attraction was Homosassa Springs, just north of Weeki Wachee. The center of a false real estate boom during the 1920s, Homosassa had floundered dramatically in the ensuing decades. Finally, in the early 1960s, some developers got hold of the springs and made them their entry in the great Florida Springs Sweepstakes.

By that time, it was hard to come up with anything new or different that would distinguish Homosassa from all the other similar spots. Fortunately, there was at least one feature that was easy to play up: for decades, Homosassa Springs had been known as "Florida's Giant Fish Bowl." A blurb elaborated on this: "Here, thousands of both fresh and salt water fish come to mingle. Visitors go below deck and 'walk underwater' in the floating observatory to view this strange mixture of fish at close hand."

The rest of Homosassa's description sounded familiar: "In the woods around the springs, friendly animals and rare birds live along the nature trails, where visitors may wander and wonder at their leisure." Homosassa's bestiary was noted for the tame squirrels that would eat right out of visitors' hands, and not-so-tame alligators that heaved themselves

The adagio became Weeki Wachee's trademark image, and was used on most souvenirs and promotional items.

out of the water to grab marshmallows. Careless tourists could find that these alligators were more than willing to eat *off* their hands rather than *out* of them!

An added feature at Homosassa, at least for a few years, was another incarnation of Ivan Tors's celebrity animal studios. Here could be seen some of the four-footed performers from Tors's recent productions: Clarence the Cross-Eyed Lion, a star of his own movie and the TV show *Daktari*, looked askance at the families who came to see him, while Judy the Chimpanzee (from the same series) caused children to go bananas. Gentle Ben was also forced to growl and bear it. It is amazing how many tourist attractions were able to display Ivan Tors's animal stars . . . but then again, most animal performances are accomplished by several look-alike beasts filling in for each other, so perhaps that explains it.

Eventually, like Wakulla and Rainbow, Homosassa Springs backed off from its attraction status and became a Florida state wildlife park. The Tors animals went on to wherever retired animal actors go, but the nature trails and the underwater observatory have been retained.

So, what is the final score on the Florida springs? Well, it looks like Silver Springs and Weeki Wachee are the only two that survive in anything resembling their original form. Rainbow Springs, Wakulla Springs, and Homosassa Springs are sterilized state parks. Apparently, even in the tourism industry—which thrives on competition—these attractions found out that their proliferation, with each offering many of the same features as the others, definitely had something fishy about it.

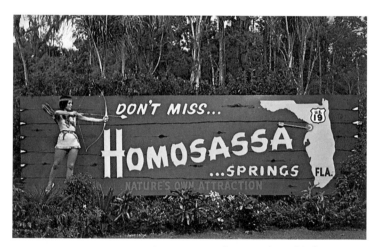

Homosassa Springs attracted attention with a miniskirted Indian princess on this "living billboard."

DC-86—Parrot Jungle, Red Road, Miami, Fla.

A Tropical Paradise in the Wild West

Everything You Came to Florida to See!

—Slogan of Floridaland

Before leaving the South's tourist attractions of the pre-Disney era, there are two remaining genres that need to be discussed. They are lumped together here not because they were connected with each other in any way, but because neither of them had any logical reason for existing in the South to begin with. Whereas most Southern attractions either capitalized on the region's place in history and myth, or were built around natural geographic features, the two categories in this chapter were, for the most part, totally manufactured environments with no connection to any version of reality.

Because the southern half of Florida was truly a jungle before Henry Flagler and his rolling-in-doughboys got their hands on it, it was at least somewhat logical that some jungle-themed attractions were developed there from the earliest days of tourism. The first wave of jungle parks were actually based on the realistic tropical nature of the region. It would take several years for the theme to sprout into something even bigger than life.

One of the first "natural" jungle attractions grew alongside U.S. 1 at Vero Beach, Florida. Industrialist Arthur McKee purchased an 80-acre hammock with the idea of expanding his already vast orange groves, but he had a change of heart when he saw the property he had bought. Impressed with the thick, natural vegetation, he decided instead to make a tropical botanical garden out of the spot. He brought in designer William Lyman Phillips, who had previously laid out the gardens at Lake Wales's Singing Tower, and soon the untamed Florida jungle began to take on some semblance of order.

Plants and trees from the tropics of other countries were brought in to give the proper atmosphere, and the McKee Jungle Gardens officially opened in 1932. The attraction remained primarily a showcase for plant life until after

World War II, when they began going after the "jungle" idea in a bigger way. Exotic animals were brought into the complex, and attractive young ladies were hired to pose in skimpy Tarzan-inspired outfits, a surefire crowd pleaser that would manifest itself in many other jungle parks in the future. Somewhat incongruously, the landscape was also dotted with some giant concrete mushrooms that would not have looked out of place on a Goofy Golf course.

McKee Jungle Gardens' later years read like a suspense novel. Like so many pre-theme park attractions, McKee's jungle was forced to close in 1976 because of declining tourist interest. The property was sold to become a condominium site, a common fate for old outdoor parks. Of the original eighty acres, all but eighteen were swallowed up by commercial development, but finally, in 1995, a group of concerned citizens got together and raised $2.1 million to purchase the remaining original part of the attraction. Efforts are underway to restore what is left of McKee Jungle Gardens, and it is hoped that someday it will be reopened, concrete mushrooms and all.

Over on the other side of Florida, George Turner was developing a six-acre plot of ground he had acquired in 1902. Turner's St. Petersburg property consisted of a sinkhole and a pond, and the entrepreneur used the fertile soil of the pond bottom to grow flowers, veg-

etables, and bananas. A plumber by trade, Turner probably considered the idea of making his sinkhole into a tourist attraction something of a pipe dream, but he plunged right in anyway. Fencing in his property, he named it Sunken Gardens and began charging admission in 1935.

George Turner's son Ralph took over the operation of Sunken Gardens in the late 1940s, and made many advances to bring it in line with other similar Florida jungle gardens. He brought in flamingoes, monkeys, and tropical birds, and eventually even made a carbon copy of Gatlinburg's Christus Gardens with his "King of Kings" exhibit, depicting the life of Christ with wax figures. But Sunken Gardens was sunk by the arrival of the high-tech theme park craze in Florida, and today most of its features have been removed. Only time will tell whether Sunken Gardens' name will be its epitaph.

Perhaps inspired by McKee Jungle Gardens and Sunken Gardens, Florida's western coast developed the very similar Sarasota Jungle Gardens in 1936. Once again, tropical plants

Stately Royal Palms, Florida

McKee Jungle Gardens was justifiably proud of its forest of royal palms, only a portion of which survives today.

and animals were the main feature, although unlike some of the other attractions, Sarasota Jungle Gardens concentrated entirely on birds rather than mammals. They were especially proud of their beautiful pink flamingoes, which, as we have seen, literally spelled "Florida" to the vast majority of souvenir-makers.

There were also attractions at which the "jungle" animals were the stars, rather than the tropical foliage. This trend dates back at least to 1933, when the Monkey Jungle opened in Miami. Their selling point was that "humans are caged and monkeys run wild." Actually, the caging was done more for the guests' protection from the mischievous primates. Here resided as many varieties of champion chimps as anyone could expect to find, and the "jungle" theme had moved one step further from reality and one step closer to its eventual tourism form. Early Florida was indeed a jungle, but monkeys were hardly natives of the region.

In 1936, Franz Scherr of Miami was fiddling with the idea of a similar jungle park where exotic birds could be seen in their natural state rather than in cages. Looking about for a suitable location, he found an undeveloped piece of property, which had previously been home to a nudist colony. Because of the colony's less-than-wholesome reputation, the landowner was willing to sell it to Scherr at any price.

Unlike some of the attractions we have seen

in previous chapters, Scherr's scheme did not necessarily entail creating the aura he was after; he only needed to enhance what was there. Trails were cleared and shrubs, flowers, and trees were planted; only then did Scherr bring in his star boarders, and Miami's famous Parrot Jungle came to life!

At first it was necessary to clip the parrots' wings to keep them from leaving their new domicile, but once they got used to it that procedure was no longer required. It seems that parrots make themselves at home quite easily, and though the neighborhoods around the attraction occasionally found some of its inhabitants visiting, the colorful celebrities always found their way back again. Both the Monkey Jungle and the Parrot Jungle continue to thrive today, proving that it is entirely possible for pioneering tourist attractions to make it in today's more competitive market, if only given the chance.

The next step in jungle attractions was to move the theme completely away from Florida's natural tropical atmosphere and strive to create a totally different world. Africa USA was one of the earliest of this type, and was operating near Boca Raton, Florida, as early as 1954. (There were other Africa USA locations; the one near Los Angeles was a longtime West Coast home for the non-Florida Ivan Tors wildlife movies and TV shows.) At this park, not only was the animal life of Africa brought in for the tourists' education, but so were some of the Dark Continent's natural features, such as waterfalls and geysers. Africa USA met an all-too-typical fate after its popularity had run its course: the property is today a housing development known as Camino Gardens.

Closely paralleling Africa USA's general appearance was Lion Country Safari, established at Palm Beach, Florida, in August 1967. Touted as the first "cageless zoo" (apparently Monkey Jungle did not count because it had only one type of animal in it), Lion Country Safari gave visitors the opportunity to drive through in their own cars, while the imported African wildlife peered at them. Visitors were warned not to lower their car windows during the drive, lest the creatures of the wild mistake them for fast food. A second Lion Country Safari location debuted just south of Atlanta in the early 1970s. The market for jungle attractions in Georgia must have left something to be desired, though, because it eventually crawled back into the underbrush and disappeared. The original Palm Beach Lion Country Safari location remains king of the jungle in its area, however.

Like many Florida attractions, Africa USA knew that pretty models wearing short shorts were a good way to bring in the customers.

GO WILD! DRIVE THRU

LION COUNTRY SAFARI

AFRICAN WILDLIFE PRESERVE

Atlanta, Georgia
22 Miles South On I-75 At Highway 138

Falling somewhere between Africa USA and Lion Country Safari, timewise, was Busch Gardens. A project of the famous Anheuser-Busch beer brewing conglomerate, the original Busch Gardens operated in Pasadena, California, between 1903 and 1928. Thirty years after this first attempt closed, the company tried it again at its brewery in Tampa, Florida. Conceived as free entertainment for those touring the brewing plant, Tampa's Busch Gardens opened in March 1959, boasting 400 exotic birds, black angus cattle, and Clydesdale horses. Its first jungle animals were almost an afterthought, appearing at the very end of the tour.

By 1966, Busch Gardens was giving places such as Africa USA a run for their money. Busch's "Monorail Safari" exposed tourists to its own growing collection of imported African wildlife, which had become its biggest claim to fame. With the dawning of the Walt Disney World theme park era in the early 1970s, Busch Gardens moved beyond the wildlife exhibits to become known as "Busch Gardens: the Dark Continent." In the years that followed, the park grew into a full-fledged Disney or Six Flags-style complex, with themed sections representing the various parts of Africa. Screaming thrill rides were added, and soon Busch Gardens' beginning as a simple wildlife exhibit

was lost in a sea of foam as thick as that on top of one of their glasses of beer.

Other jungle attractions battled for survival of the fittest. Down in Naples, Florida, Jungle Larry's Safari followed the pattern of putting the tourists in with the animals and seeing who was more interested in whom. Like Africa USA, Jungle Larry's was part of a chain of such parks across the country. Their owner was veteran bush whacker "Jungle Larry" Tetzlaff, who had been associated with a number of other menageries, including the St. Augustine Alligator Farm and Ross Allen's Reptile Institute at Silver Springs. Tetzlaff won some measure of

JUNGLE LARRY
EXPEDITION in the AMAZON JUNGLES
Color Book

fame by virtue of his guest appearances on various TV programs, and in 1969 brought his "safari" to Florida's Caribbean Gardens. The explorer departed this earth for regions unknown in 1984, but his jungle park is still doing a roaring business under the direction of his wife and sons.

It might seem that the Great Smoky Mountains would be the last place on earth to look for jungle animals, but have you forgotten about Pigeon Forge's Fort Weare Game Park, at which we took a peek back in chapter 4? In later years, this collection of furry, four-footed friends changed its name to Jungle Cargo, which sounds more like a label on a shipping crate than a place you would actually visit. Obviously tourists felt the same way, because Jungle Cargo was finally returned to sender.

The final, and ultimate, development in jungle attractions came about when some owners decided to pull out all the stops, completely ignore Florida's geographic location, and go for the jugular with a total Polynesian, South Seas island look. If tourists wanted jungles, brother, they were gonna get 'em! Tiki Gardens, between Clearwater and St. Petersburg, strove to create "a bit of Polynesia" in the Florida wilderness, complete with thatched missionary huts and replicas of tribal statues. Its influence spread, and today there are scores of Florida motels, gift shops, and restaurants that strive for the look of the South Pacific rather than either of the bodies of water that actually touch the state's coastline.

Another example erupted along Panama City Beach's Miracle Strip in 1966. For several years, Silver Springs' famous snake doctor Ross Allen had been operating a small zoo adjacent to the gaudy Miracle Strip Amusement Park, but the zoo's attendance was not really what anyone had expected it to be. To this spot in 1965 came Vincent "Val" Valentine, a commercial artist and former cartoon animator from Ocala, who had created artwork for nearly every one of the central Florida attractions. (It was he who had built the Santa's sleigh and Toonerville Trolley rides for Silver Springs' Deer Ranch and Carriage Cavalcade, respectively.) Valentine bought Allen's Panama City Beach wildlife collection, and set about making it more alluring to passersby.

He accomplished this with a little roadside trick called "packaging." Valentine erected a towering artificial volcano on the site of the former zoo, and dubbed his new attraction Jungle Land. The "volcano" spewed smoke and flame from its crater continuously, and was a

see TIKI GARDENS 'South Sea Island Paradise In Florida' and visit 7 FASCINATING SHOPS TRADER FRANK'S RESTAURANT Thrill to Our Age Old "Torch Lighting Ceremony" FREE each evening at twilight weather permitting SEE OUR BIG GARDEN - ALIVE WITH BEAUTIFUL PEACOCKS AND POLYNESIAN LORE - ADMISSION CHARGED Big Garden Open Daily 9 a.m. - Sunset Shops Open Daily 9 a.m. - 9:30 p.m. 196th Ave. & Gulf Blvd., Indian Rocks Beach real attention-grabber at night. Local bathing beauties donned Sheena of the Jungle attire to help pull in that particular class of customer...although sometimes they got so carried away with their act that they almost crossed the line into looking like prehistoric *One Million Years B.C.* cavegirl types rather than jungle denizens.

Jungle Land was a big hit on the Miracle Strip, at least for several years. Changing tastes, and a "maturing" of the strip's attractions, eventually spelled its end, however. In the late 1970s Jungle Land was dismantled, but what was to be done with the volcano? Fortunately, in this case demolition was not the final solution. A chain of Florida souvenir stores, Alvin's Island, constructed a small shopping center around the volcano's base and renamed it Alvin's Magic Mountain Mall. Although the smoke and fire have had their belch squelched, the volcano crater continues to protrude from the mall's roof.

The other major subgenre of attractions was a type that fit the South even less than the jungle attractions did. Beginning in the early 1960s, tourists found a veritable bonanza of wild Wild West-themed amusement parks holding down the fort in every major resort center. At first there was a constant wagon train of automobiles winding its way across the happy trails and the big valleys to these parks, and it looked like the attractions were all in high chaparral. However, when the gunsmoke finally cleared, all but a very few of them had been sent to tombstone territory.

More than any other type of attraction, the Western parks were born and died strictly because of television. When the TV Western reached the zenith of its popularity in the late 1950s and early 1960s, the tourist industry responded in a way that has rarely been seen since. Never before had so many similar attractions

Val Valentine's smoking volcano at Panama City Beach's Jungle Land.

opened in such a short period of time; likewise, seldom did so many shut down their ticket booths almost simultaneously.

It must be pointed out here that the Western park did not have its beginnings in the South. The grandpappy of them all was California's Knott's Berry Farm, which started its own "ghost town" back in the 1940s. Knott's stated purpose was to recreate for its visitors what a typical such town in early California was like. The Southern renditions of the Old West, by contrast, were based totally on the media's representations of the era. Trying to pinpoint just which Western park was the first in the South is a daunting task. What is known is that, in 1960–61, at least three parks began developing the theme to varying degrees.

The Tweetsie Railroad, near Blowing Rock, North Carolina, long predated the public's fascination with Westerns. An actual railroad at one time, Tweetsie got its unusual name from the shrill, piping sound of its whistle. It served as the major transportation through the rugged mountain country between Boone, North Carolina, and Johnson City, Tennessee, from the end of the Civil War to the coming of paved highways. The rail line fell into disuse after that, and in 1940 a flood washed away most of what was left of the track.

Into Tweetsie's picture rode singing cowboy hero Gene Autry, who wanted to put the locomotive back in the saddle again. North Carolina interests persuaded the crooning cowpoke to sell Tweetsie back to them, so it could be restored to operation in the region it had served so well. A cowboy never goes back on his word, so, in the late 1950s, Tweetsie came under the ownership of those tycoons of the Southern mountain attractions, Grover and Harry Robbins. Three years of work on Tweetsie resulted in a three-mile circular track around Roundhouse Mountain. However, at the time of Tweetsie's reopening, nothing was said about a Western town going along with it. The railroad was the whole show until 1961.

In that year, Tweetsie Junction was opened as the railroad's "home base." It contained the elements that would become familiar to patrons of all future Western parks: there was the train ride itself, which was interrupted by attacking bands of Indians and other marauding ornery owlhoots; staged gunfights on the town street; a "saloon" with live entertainment; and so forth. For a while, the honorary sheriff of Tweetsie

The Jungle Land volcano today, as the titular feature of Alvin's Magic Mountain Mall.

A crowd of city slickers watches the marshal preserve law and order at Ghost Town in the Sky.

was the original could be debated until Roy Rogers shoots Hopalong Cassidy in cold blood. One thing that did make Ghost Town in the Sky unique among Western attractions is that (gasp!) its visitors did not ride a train to get to its entrance gate. The park got its name because it was perched high atop a "mile-high" mountain, so the traditional locomotive loop had to be replaced with a choice of chairlift (shades of Gatlinburg!) or incline (shades of Lookout Mountain!).

Otherwise, Ghost Town in the Sky resembled most of the others. The Marshal found it necessary to gun down a collection of slimy sidewinders several times daily (often the *same ones* more than once!), with the somewhat mercenary help of "Digger the Undertaker." Afterward, everyone could whoop it up at the Red Dog Saloon, where the usual bevy of can-can dancers could be found kicking up their heels and their skirts. An amusement park section, with traditional carnival-type rides, filled out the property. And *that,* pilgrims, is where the ubiquitous train ride finally put in its belated appearance.

The Robbins brothers, who had revitalized the Tweetsie Railroad and would later give the world North Carolina's incarnation of the Land of Oz on Beech Mountain, struck it rich again in Pigeon Forge, Tennessee, in 1961. You must recall that at that time, the centennial of the

Junction was an ex-children's TV show host from Charlotte, Fred Kirby, whose presence served to reinforce the park's ties to television. Later, amusement rides were added on the top of "Magic Mountain," the locale of the dreaded Castle of the Sleeping Giant we saw in chapter 5. Tweetsie Railroad continues to run today, one of only two of the Western park pardners that have survived the years with their original theme intact.

The other present-day survivor is the Ghost Town in the Sky at Maggie Valley, North Carolina, founded by R. B. Coburn. Construction of this Western setting also began in 1960, with a 1961 opening date, so whether it or Tweetsie

Civil War was quite a big deal, especially in the South. Grover and Harry Robbins borrowed a historical page from themselves, and built a park they named the Rebel Railroad. Basically it was a Pigeon Forge recreation of Tweetsie, with the steam train running past a general store, saloon, and the like.

Once the centennial furor had subsided, the Rebel Railroad began moving away from its Confederate roots and leaning more and more toward its eventual Western theme. The name of the park became Goldrush Junction, while the promotional literature reached a new frenzy of enthusiasm: "Ride the famous Goldrush, Pigeon Forge, Gatlinburg, and Western, pulled by Klondike Katie, the 70-ton locomotive brought all the way from the Alaskan Gold Fields where it once hauled miners over the White Pass and Yukon Route from Skagway to Whitehorse! Take an exciting five-mile trip through the wild, wild west where Indian attacks and train robberies still happen every trip." Sound familiar?

Many people who pay no attention to tourism's legacy are surprised to learn that what was once the relatively obscure Goldrush Junction is today one of Pigeon Forge's most famous features. In 1977, Goldrush changed hands and names again, becoming the Tennessee arm of Missouri's famous Silver Dollar City attraction. It was in 1986 that Silver Dollar City joined forces with country music bombshell Dolly Parton, and the former Rebel Railroad/Goldrush Junction/ Silver Dollar City property became known to all as Dollywood, which it remains to this day. As such, it has deserted its Western angle, and is directed toward recreating Ms. Parton's impoverished childhood in the Great Smokies and her later rise to fame.

There was really no logical reason for the aforementioned Western parks to become so entrenched in the Southern mountains, unless one counts the somewhat appropriate geography of the area. But the mountain-country Western towns looked positively at home compared to their counterparts that eventually sprang up in Florida (where else?!).

The first two to develop in the inappropriately tropical setting of Florida came about almost simultaneously along Panama City Beach's Miracle Strip. Both started out slowly, and then bloomed into carbon copies of each other. The process began in 1960, when Goofy Golf magnate Lee Koplin leased some adjoining property to two different concessionaires. One was a train ride, the other a sky ride. Neither went anywhere. Oh, the sky ride went

WESTERN CAROLINA'S
GHOST TOWN
IN THE SKY!
at
GHOST MOUNTAIN PARK
ON US-19 BETWEEN CHEROKEE AND ASHEVILLE, N. C.

RIDE THE INCLINE RAILWAY—CHAIR LIFT
OR TROLLEY BUSES TO GHOST TOWN
MAGGIE VALLEY U.S. 19
IN THE SMOKY MOUNTAINS

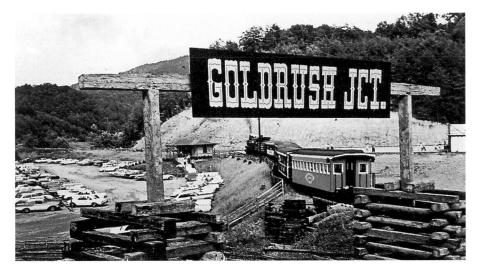

Pigeon Forge hit the mother lode with Goldrush Junction in the 1960s.

somewhere, all right: to the end of its cable and back. Koplin's son Randy explains that the whole appeal of the sky ride has to be explained by the era in which it operated. In 1960 there were no two-story buildings on the beach, so a ride 100 feet in the air gave visitors a view that was unobtainable anywhere else. The train ride did make stops in a wooded area behind the Goofy Golf course, where other individuals operated a storybook park known as the Magic Forest (rather like an outdoor version of Fairyland Caverns) and a deer ranch not unlike Tommy Bartlett's. Meanwhile, a couple of miles down the strip, the Churchwell family, who were still operating Panama City's first attraction, the Long Beach Resort, also started a train ride to nowhere.

Both entertainment complexes could see that they needed something more to entertain their train passengers. It is not recorded whether Lee Koplin was paying any attention to what was going on in the North Carolina and Tennessee mountains, but in 1963 he ditched the deer ranch and Magic Forest, and replaced them with his own Western town, which became known as Tombstone Territory (named after a popular TV Western of the late 1950s). Koplin's considerable talents at concrete sculpture, as evidenced by his miniature golf courses, came into play at Tombstone, where he built an authentic-looking Spanish mission and various statues to give the place some charm. Other buildings were appropriately rustic in appearance, except for the fact that their exteriors were surfaced with cypress wood . . . a building material that was no doubt scarce in the real western United States.

Down at Long Beach Resort, the Churchwells took note of what was shaping up at Tombstone Territory, and this spurred them into action themselves. They constructed an even larger Western town at the halfway point of their railroad's circle. Since Koplin had named his town after a TV show, they felt they could get away with the same thing, but what should it be called? Ah, but one of the Churchwells was a good friend of the crusty old actor Edgar Buchanan, who was enjoying great fame for his role as Uncle Joe in the successful television comedy *Petticoat Junction*. Never mind that the TV Petticoat Junction had nothing to do with the West at all; it spotlighted a train, and that was enough! Buchanan helped the Churchwells obtain the proper permission, and soon the name was being applied to the new attraction at Long Beach Resort. Because there was a large open space between the railroad depot and the "ghost town," amusement rides were added to grab the attention of passersby.

Now the competition got really ferocious. Petticoat Junction was larger than Tombstone Territory, and spent far more money on advertising and promotion, so Lee Koplin fought back in the way he knew best. The spot next to U.S. 98 from which his locomotive and sky ride departed was somewhat nondescript, with only a small depot for decoration. Concrete to the rescue! Koplin built giant roadside lures to round up stray tourists. His masterpiece was a gigantic cave containing an adobe Indian village. Housed within the village were souvenir shops selling "authentic" Indian wares imported from Cherokee, North Carolina, and a stage area in which Indian-style pageants could be performed. But Koplin didn't stop there. With welding torch and concrete spreader working overtime, he built a towering Indian statue holding the attraction's sign, a pair of

MAGIC FOREST
•Visit Enchanted Castle •Cross Swinging Bridge •Ride Jungle River Boat •See Animated Wild Animals •Enjoy Beautiful Scenery •Stay As Long As You Like •Catch A Later Train At No Extra Fare

Don't Miss It

35¢
to all

Florida's Newest Attraction
SKYRIDE
Prices Reduced
50¢ TO ALL RE-RIDES **25¢**

ON U.S. 98   WEST PANAMA CITY BEACH, FLORIDA

These early 1960s attractions were the beginning of Panama City Beach's Tombstone Territory.

longhorn cattle, a totem pole, several cacti, and, for some reason, a giant genie emerging from Aladdin's lamp, with a set of metal stairs leading up to his outstretched hand for a photo opportunity. The place couldn't be missed.

One has a vision of the ultimate outcome of this competition: a dusty Western street, with the cowboys of Tombstone Territory at one end and the cowboys of Petticoat Junction at the other, facing each other in a *High Noon*-style shootout. ("This resort ain't big enough fer the both of us!") But this never had to take place. Time, a force more inescapable than Marshal Dillon, had its own effect on both attractions. The Tombstone Territory sky ride was effectively put out of commission in 1975 when Hurricane Eloise scattered its dangling buckets far and wide. Since it had been seeing less and less use anyway, the machinery was allowed to rust into picturesque decay. By 1979, the train ride to Tombstone Territory had made its final

Main Street, Tombstone Territory. The hombre in the black coat is Goofy Golf impresario Lee Koplin.

At Panama City Beach's Petticoat Junction, it appears that Bobbie Jo, Billie Jo, and Betty Jo have turned to a life of crime and are holding up engineer Floyd Smoot. So, where's Uncle Joe? He's movin' kinda slow at the Junction.

run, and the giant concrete figures sat by the roadside, staring out to sea with sightless eyes.

Petticoat Junction was also hearing a discouraging word. Whereas its location at Long Beach Resort had once been the center of the Panama City Beach strip, that center had been gradually shifting to the west, and now few people even made it to Petticoat's junction. The 1970 cancellation of the TV show for which it was named also did not help matters any. On Labor Day 1984, the trains stopped running, the stores and other buildings were boarded up, their contents and the amusement rides were auctioned off, and the park became as much a part of history as the Old West era it depicted. Today, a Wal-Mart superstore sits on its former site. As for Tombstone Territory, its roadside section, where the concrete giants hung out, is a string of fast-food restaurants. The Western town itself still stands, to a certain extent,

slowly rotting behind a chain-link fence in a wooded area.

While Tombstone and Petticoat were shooting it out along the Gulf beaches, down in Ocala the biggest and most elaborate Western park of them all rode out of the stockade in 1963. Six Gun Territory was conceived by R. B. Coburn, the hombre who had brought Ghost Town in the Sky to life in North Carolina. But in Florida, much more property was available than had been on the mountaintop in the Smokies, and as a result Six Gun Territory was spread out over some 254 vast acres. Its proximity to Silver Springs gave it the oomph it needed to draw in customers, and more than likely the majority of those customers were unfamiliar with its predecessors in the mountain country.

That was good, because apart from its enormous size, Six Gun was a clone of Ghost Town. In fact, in photographs it is practically impossible to tell the two apart. Six Gun even featured the same cast of characters (including Digger the Undertaker), and its "live saloon show" photos were pretty near interchangeable with those of Ghost Town. Six Gun did have a much larger "town" portion, complete with a village square, and its buildings generally appeared to be more elaborate and permanent. As for its roadside look, Six Gun seemed to borrow heavily from its Miracle Strip cousins.

Yes, it had its own sky ride and locomotive trip, and the main feature of the entrance was a huge concrete mountain that may or may not have been inspired by Koplin's focal point at Tombstone Territory.

We have all heard it said often that the bigger they are the harder they fall. Six Gun Territory was eventually defeated by its own tremendous bulk, especially when it began feeling the crunch from the arrival of Walt Disney World. The overhead was just too great, and the decline and disappearance of TV Westerns sent it to the last roundup. In September 1978, Six Gun Territory was put up for sale. Could anyone have been expected to buy it with an eye to continuing to operate it as a Western park? Don't make me chuckle! It was indeed sold, but what is occupying its space today? A shopping mall. What is the name of the mall? You had better sit down for this one . . . Six Gun Plaza. And so, the Old West lives on. . . .

TOMBSTONE TERRITORY

Ride The Iron Horse To Tombstone Ter...

Into the Past
WHERE ENTERTAINMENT IS FREE!

Next to Goofy Golf

W. Panama City Beach

Giant concrete statues were Tombstone Territory's ammunition in the ongoing competition with Petticoat Junction.

R. B. Coburn had one more Western park

to develop before he hung up his spurs. This time, he returned to the area where he started, and took over a small park in Cherokee, North Carolina, which bore the lame name of Cherokee Wonderland. About all it had to offer the little buckaroos was a sky ride and train trip, but when Coburn got his brands on it, that changed. Soon, visitors to Cherokee were treated to his latest vision of the past: Frontier Land!

You say it makes sense to find such a park in Cherokee, since Indians were always a big part of any Western attraction? But wait—aren't the Indians usually portrayed as the villains of the dramas? And isn't Cherokee a genuine Indian reservation, where logically they would be the good guys? And what about Frontier Land's press release:

Frontier Land has brought the days of our early frontier back to life. The ghosts of Daniel Boone, Davy Crockett, and many others are lurking in Fort Cherokee, which was built to protect the little town of Pioneer Junction from the hostile redmen in Indian Territory. A constant atmosphere of conflict and excitement prevails in Frontier Land [with the attraction surrounded by real Native Americans, we just bet it did!!]. The cafeteria in Pioneer Junction can provide you with full-course meals, hot dogs, hamburgers, barbecue, and soft drinks [fare that was probably as scarce as cypress wood in the early West]. One admission price includes a ride on the authentic wood-burning 1860 train, a beautiful ride on the Gondola Sky Ride, an Indian attack on the pioneers and soldiers every hour throughout the day ["It's one o'clock, Colonel, guess it's time fer the Indians to be attackin' us again!"], Indian dancing, stage shows, and the Last Chance Saloon ["Daddy, haven't we been to this place before?"].

At least the pioneers and soldiers at Fort Cherokee could be secure in the knowledge that the Indians were going to attack them once every hour; it was much easier to be prepared that way. But nothing could prepare these delightfully hokey attractions for the changes in the public's attitude, and Frontier Land started pushing up daisies in 1983. The site then became a water park, which also eventually bit the dust. Today the property is the location for Cherokee's grand Harrah's Casino. Hmm, you know, it looks like the Indians won the final battle there after all.

And now, we come to the climax...the pay-off...the Grand Finale! If you have struggled this far, you should have gathered that the South contained any variety of tacky tourist trap that could be studied up to make people part with some of their Yankee dollahs. But, when all is said and done, which attraction could be awarded the prize as the absolute tackiest... the most mercenary...the most calculated... the one that outdid all the rest when it came to pure, unadulterated, shameless hokum? The envelope, please. And the winner is... that capsulization of everything that was Dixie

before Disney, the one and only *Floridaland*!!

What? You haven't heard of Floridaland? Don't feel too inferior...many others haven't either. But, in its day, Floridaland was one of the most aggressive advertisers in the entire South. This fifty-acre park was located on U.S. 41, which you will recall as the faithful old Dixie Highway, between Sarasota and Venice. Never had another attraction tried to pack every possible element of the Southern roadside scene into one place, and make tourists feel that they were being done a favor. Even its slogan, "Everything You Came to Florida to See!," gave visitors a hint as to its bombastic nature.

Floridaland heavily advertised its "Ten Big

Although not strictly an amusement park, this restaurant in Clewiston, Florida, staked out its own claim in the great Western attraction roundup.

Attractions," which read like a list of the rest of the South, from Virginia to Miami: (1) Porpoise Show; (2) Ghost Town; (3) Can Can Show; (4) Deer Park; (5) Gardens; (6) Whiskey Still; (7) Goat Mountain; (8) Indian Village; (9) Tour Trains; and (10) Sea Lions. The advertising played up the Western theme more than any of the others, but included photographs that looked positively surreal: a porpoise show in a jungle/Polynesian setting . . . a moonshiner and his still, looking like they'd been transplanted from Pigeon Forge . . . flowering pathways that looked like a poor man's Cypress Gardens. . . .

Sure, Floridaland was tacky. So, in a way, were many of the pre-theme park attractions in the South. But they were relics of their time . . . a time when getting there was indeed half the fun, and the more that could be seen during those long drives between destinations, the better.

That was what highway travel was all about in those days.

That was what it was like in Dixie . . . before Disney.

Floridaland embodied everything that is included in the phrase "Dixie Before Disney."

Epilogue

Lookin' back on things, the view always improves.

—Walt Kelly

So...with our comfortable hindsight, what more can we say to summarize the story of Southern tourist attractions? What can they tell us about society...and about ourselves?

Well, for one thing, there was one important attitude that ran through all of the attractions discussed in this book. That attitude was one of *fun*. Sure, they were all in business to make money, and most of them did that very well. But there was something about them all that went beyond that. It was financially necessary that they make themselves infinitely appealing and compelling to a wide variety of people. As we have seen, many of them succeeded at this for decades, but others were unable to sustain visitor interest for more than a few years.

A friend of mine who teaches high school in Texas recently told me about one of his students who returned from her summer vacation with the report that she and her family had visited Walt Disney World. When he asked her how she liked the park, she replied that it was okay at first, but that after a couple of hours she was bored. That one statement may tell us a lot. When attitudes have gotten to the point that boredom sets in after only a couple of hours at a place like Walt Disney World, something has gone wrong somewhere.

The Wild West parks...Silver Springs...Rock City and its Fairyland Caverns...the Confederama...the hillbilly and Indian attractions of the Great Smoky Mountains...the observation towers...all of these came out of an era when the very idea of being someplace different was all that was needed to keep visitors entertained. Call it naivete if you will...maybe even innocence...but at one time people did not expect so much out of their vacation destinations. The prevailing attitude nowadays seems to be a resigned "Let's get this over with," rather than an anticipatory "What can we do today?"

While doing research for this book, I had occasion to revisit the Goofy Golf course in Panama City Beach for the first time in many years. It was the off season, so few people were around. One thing that caught my attention was a couple of small children whose mother had brought them to the course. They knew nothing about the game of miniature golf, but the gigantic, brightly colored statuary was making a definite impression on them. Back and forth they ran, peering at the concrete denizens of the course and working themselves into an absolute fit of excitement. It occurred to me that here before my eyes was living proof that the things that entertained children and their parents forty years ago can still do so today...if only we can manage to see them with an open and unclouded mind.

Has the old attitude been lost forever? Maybe, but maybe not. It is up to *us*. Should we allow ourselves to become so cynical and pseudosophisticated that we cannot revel in the corniest activities, admiring them simply because they *are* so unsophisticated? Try looking at these old attractions through the eyes you had as a child, when the world around you was brand new and gift-wrapped, and see what a difference that makes. You might be surprised at what you have been missing.

"Happy Motoring!"

Bibliographical Essays

General Information

When I began working on *Dixie Before Disney* in earnest in the autumn of 1995, my first inclination was to look up any previous books that had been published dealing with Southern tourism. I quickly made an important discovery: there weren't any. This came as a sort of shock, rather like being unexpectedly pushed into the path of an oncoming truck. However, I decided to sweat it out, and now you have been able to enjoy the product of my perspiring palms. There were, and are, other books that deal with the subject of tourism in America, even some that touch upon the South itself, and anyone interested in the subject is encouraged to seek these out. In no particular order, the volumes that contributed to this one in a more general (rather than specific, as detailed below) way include: *Weird Wonderful America* by Laura A. Bergheim (New York: Tilden Press, 1988); *Highways to Heaven: The Auto-Biography of America* by Christopher Finch (New York: HarperCollins Publishers, 1992); *Main Street to Miracle Mile: American Roadside Architecture* by Chester H. Liebs (Baltimore: Johns Hopkins University Press, 1995); *Fun Along the Road: American Tourist Attractions* by John Margolies (Boston: Bullfinch Press, 1998); *U.S. 1: America's Original Main Street* by Andrew H. Malcolm (New York: St. Martin's Press, 1991); *The Encyclopedia of Bad Taste* by Jane and Michael Stern (New York: HarperCollins Publishers, 1990); *Route 66: The Mother Road* by Michael Wallis (New York: St. Martin's Press, 1990); *The New Roadside America* by Mike Wilkins, Ken Smith, and Doug Kirby (New York: Simon & Schuster, 1992); *The Encyclopedia of Southern Culture,* edited by Charles Reagan Wilson and William Ferris (New York: Anchor Books, 1989); *Hitting the Road: The Art of the American Road Map* by Douglas A. Yorke Jr., John Margolies, and Eric Baker (San Francisco: Chronicle Books, 1996); *The Motel in America* by John A. Jakle, Keith A. Sculle, and Jefferson S. Rogers (Baltimore: Johns Hopkins University Press, 1996); *Route 66 Remembered* by Michael Karl Witzel (Osceola, Wis.: Motorbooks International, 1996); *Mid-Atlantic Roadside Delights* by Will Anderson (Portland, Me.: Anderson & Sons, 1991); *The Lincoln Highway: Main Street Across America* by Drake Hokanson (Iowa City: University of Iowa Press, 1988); *Way Out West* by Jane and Michael Stern (New York: HarperCollins, 1993); *California Crazy: Roadside Vernacular Architecture* by Jim Heimann and Rip Georges (San Francisco: Chronicle Books, 1980);

New England Roadside Delights by Will Anderson (Portland, Me.: Anderson & Sons, 1989); *The Well-Built Elephant and Other Roadside Attractions* by J. J. C. Andrews (New York: Congdon & Weed, 1984); *Americans on the Road: From Autocamp to Motel* by Warren Belasco (Cambridge: The MIT Press, 1979); *Googie's: California Coffee Shop Architecture* by Alan Hess (San Francisco: Chronicle Books, 1985); *The Tourist: Travel in 20th Century North America* by John Jackle (Lincoln: University of Nebraska Press, 1985); *The End of the Road: Vanishing Highway Architecture in America* by John Margolies (New York: Penguin Books, 1981); *The Colossus of Roads: Myth & Symbol along the American Highway* by Karal Ann Marling (Minneapolis: University of Minnesota Press, 1984); *Open Road: A Celebration of the American Highway* by Phil Patton (New York: Simon & Schuster, 1986); *U.S. 40: A Roadside of the American Experience* by Thomas J. Schlereth (Indianapolis: Indiana Historical Society, 1985); *Route 66: The Highway and Its People* by Quinta Scott and Susan Croce Kelly (Norman: University of Oklahoma Press, 1988); *Coney Island: A Postcard Journey to the City of Fire* by Richard Snow (New York: Brightwaters Press, 1984); *Inventing New England: Regional Tourism in the 19th Century* by Dona Brown (Washington, D.C.: Smithsonian Institute Press, 1997); *The Romance of Reunion: Northerners & the South, 1865–1900* by Nina Sibler (Chapel Hill: University of North Carolina Press, 1993); and *U.S. 40 Today* by Thomas and Geraldine Vale (Madison: University of Wisconsin Press, 1983). A couple of vintage guidebooks were also helpful in determining dates and locations: *A Guide to Florida Vacations* (Tallahassee: Florida Development Commission, 1961) and *Discover All of Florida* (Tallahassee: Florida Development Commission, 1966). A most valuable publication for anyone dealing with roadside history is the *SCA Journal,* published by the Society for Commercial Archeology. All information not cited below came from my own personal memories, photograph collection, and collection of travel memorabilia (often referred to as "junk").

Chapter 1

For information on the pre-automobile era of Southern tourism, I rode through *Florida from the Beginning to 1992,* by William S. Coker and Jerrell H. Shofner (Houston: Pioneer Publications, 1991) and *Florida: A Place in the Sun* by Heinz Erhardt and Al Burt (Offenburg, West Germany: Dr. Franz Burda, 1974). The best source I could dig up for the story of the early highway system in the South was Howard Lawrence Preston's *Dirt Roads to Dixie* (Knoxville: University of Tennessee Press, 1991). Additional details on the Dixie Highway came from "Driving the Dixie: The Development of the Dixie Highway Corridor" by Martha Carver, in the *SCA News Journal* (Fall/Winter 1994-95). Less has been written about the post-1926 period in highway development, but details on some of the latter-day numbered routes to the South were gleaned from Hal Foust's "What 3 Routes to South Offer Vacationeers" (*Chicago Daily Tribune*, December 17, 1954), Wynola Robison's "Survey Finds Interstate Not Hurting Route 41" (*Chattanooga Times*, April 11, 1962), and Virginia Van Der Veer Hamilton's "Before the Freeway, There Was U.S. 11" (*The New York Times*, November 23, 1986). To date, the only major documentation of the early Alabama roadside attraction known as The Bottle is "All That's Left of The Bottle Is Name" by Mike Bolton, in an undated clipping from *The Birmingham News*. Alfred Eisenstaedt's "Hospitable Land for a Tour in Springtime" (*Life*, April 25, 1960) was proof positive that the South had become a true vacation destination for the entire United States. Roadside advertising has been well documented in two coffee table books, *Rock City Barns: A Passing Era* by David B. Jenkins (Chattanooga: Free Spirit Press, 1996) and *See Rock City Barns: A Tennessee Tradition* by Anita Armstrong Capps (Lookout Mtn., Ga.: A. A. Capps, 1996). Most of the information on the development of the Florida Welcome Stations came from an interview with Brian Rheawinkel of the Florida Department of Tourism, and the Florida stations' successors in other states were described by Bill Hardman of the Southeastern Tourism Bureau. The long and bitter debate over the number and placement of billboards has produced many reams of newspaper coverage, but for this book's purposes, Jack Steele's article "Senate Nears Showdown on Billboards," from an undated (but early 1960s) clipping from the *Knoxville (Tenn.) News* was the most helpful. Maxine Thompson's wonderfully sentimental tribute to the decline of roadside advertising, "Remember When Every Barn Had Its SEE ROCK CITY Sign?" appeared in the April 1973 issue of *Georgia* magazine, and Ann Elstad of that publication granted permission for the excerpt used here. Finally, a complete chronology of the development of Walt Disney World can be found in Bob Thomas's *Walt Disney: An American Original* (New York: Pocket Books, 1976).

Chapter 2

For the history of Stuckey's, I had very little help from the Stuckey's Corporation itself, but did manage to meet with the exceedingly friendly Bill Stuckey Jr. to fill in some of the empty pecan shells in that company's past. Additional Stuckey's trivia came from two articles, "The Pecan Candy Man" (*Southern Living*, February 1966) and "Teal Roofs & Pecan Logs: A History of Stuckey's Pecan Shoppes" by Lisa Raflo and Jeffrey Durbin (*SCA Journal*, Fall 1995). The story of Stuckey's chief competitor, Horne's, was a bit more difficult since that company disintegrated so many years ago. Bill Stuckey Jr. was helpful in establishing Bob Horne's association with Stuckey's, but most of the early Horne's data came from Jim Antone of Bayard, Florida, who at the time operated an antique mall in the former original Horne's motel. For the story of the third candy shoppe chain, Saxon's, I conducted a lengthy interview with the delightful Cora Saxon herself, and for additional info she gave me a copy of the article "Saxon Candy Story of 'Rags to Riches'" by George Smith, published in the *Anniston (Ala.) Star*, August 14, 1977. For the yummy story of Colonel Sanders and his days as a restaurateur in Corbin, Kentucky, the prime authority turned out to be the goateed one's own autobiography, *Finger Lickin' Good* (Carol Stream, Ill.: Creation House, 1974). The purchase and eventual restoration of the original Sanders' Cafe in Corbin is well documented in Wallace Hebert's *A Year to Restore, A Year to Remember*. (Columbia, Tenn.: JRN, Inc., 1990). I had to devour several volumes to get the whole enchilada concerning the other restaurant chains that began in the South, but the most helpful tomes were John Mariani's *America Eats Out* (New York: William Morrow & Co., 1991), Philip Langdon's *Orange Roofs, Golden Arches* (New York: Alfred A. Knopf, 1986), Jeffrey Tennyson's *Hamburger Heaven* (New York: Hyperion, 1993), and Michael Karl Witzel's *The American Drive-In* (Osceola, Wis.: Motorbooks International, 1994). The story of Kemmons Wilson and the beginnings of Holiday Inn came partially from an interview conducted with Wilson by the ABC television network in 1985, but also from *Home Away from Home: Motels in America* by John Margolies (Boston: Bullfinch Press, 1995) and *Symbols of America* by Hal Morgan (New York: Penguin Books, 1986), which went into some detail on the history of the classic Holiday Inn "Great Sign." Mom-and-Pop motels in the South have been documented in John Baeder's *Gas, Food, & Lodging* (New York: Abbeville Press, 1982) and James B. Jones's paper *The Development of Motor Tourism in Tennessee's Southeastern Corridor, 1910–1945* (Nashville: Tennessee Historical Commission, 1991). Also helpful was the compilation "Pre-War Motel Listings" by Arthur Krim, in the *SCA News Journal* (Winter 1990). Warren H. Anderson, in his book *Vanishing Roadside America* (Tucson: University of Arizona Press, 1981) was one of the first to explore the "misplaced" phenomenon among roadside businesses, a subject that was also dealt with in Douglas Towne's article "The Mysteries of the Wandering Cactus Unearthed" in the *SCA Journal* (Spring/Summer 1995). The most complete discussion of the Wigwam Village motel chain is a chapter in

Roadside America (Ames: Iowa State University Press, 1990), edited by Jan Jennings. Most of the motel and restaurant listings found here stem from my own collection of postcards and tourist literature, but one article that proved to be helpful was "Try Aunt Fanny's Cabin" (*Southern Living*, May 1966). My own research into the chain of Lum's restaurants can be found in the article "Lum & Abner and the Great American Roadside: Lum's Restaurants" in *The Jot 'Em Down Journal* (February 1996). For those interested in the third leg of the food-lodging-gas trilogy, I recommend John Margolies' *Pump & Circumstance: Glory Days of the Gas Station.* (Boston: Bullfinch Press, 1993) and Michael Karl Witzel's *The American Gas Station* (Osceola, Wis.: Motorbooks International, 1992). *Signs of Our Time* by Margolies and Emily Gwathney (New York: Abbeville Press, 1993) and Patricia Buckley's "Jumbo Oranges & Giant Lemons" (*SCA Journal*, Spring/Summer 1995) are also good general references for roadside oddities. The amount of data that has been published regarding souvenirs is minuscule (and so are many of the souvenirs), but two books that treat the subject with obvious love and respect are *Coast to Coast: The Best of Travel Decal Art* by Rod Dyer, Brad Benedict, and David Lees (New York: Abbeville Press, 1991), and Nancy McMichael's *Snowdomes* (New York: Abbeville Press, 1990). Professor Charles Reagan Wilson waxed eloquent about his personal souvenir collection in Bob Carlton's article "Southern Tacky" (*The Birmingham News*, May 7, 1995). Needless to say, the authoritative source for information on the Dick Huddleston Store in Pine Ridge, Arkansas, is the National Lum and Abner Society, and a complete discussion of Huddleston's activities appears in my own article "The Country Merchant" (*The Jot 'Em Down Journal*, August 1986).

Chapter 3

Two of the works cited for chapter 1 also provided grains of truth (and grains of sand) for the development of Florida's beaches: *Florida from the Beginning to 1992* by William S. Coker and Jerrell H. Shofner (Houston: Pioneer Publications, 1991) and *Florida: A Place in the Sun* by Heinz Erhardt and Al Burt (Offenburg, West Germany: Dr. Franz Burda, 1974). More details on both coasts came from Jack Kofoed's *The Florida Story* (New York: Doubleday & Co., 1960), and a lengthy interview with Dwight Wilson of the Jacksonville Beach Historical Society answered some questions about the Atlantic side of Florida. Marineland provided quite a bit of historical data on itself, including the unpublished 1984 paper titled *Historical Portion of National Register Nomination for Marineland of Florida.* Carole Griffin of the Miami Seaquarium and Steve Petermann of the Gulfarium made sure their histories did not become waterlogged.

"Moviemaking Moves South" (*Southern Living*, April 1967) spun the scenario of the Ivan Tors movie studio in southern Florida. The same magazine devoted an article to MGM's *Bounty* exhibit ("You Can Visit the *Bounty* at St. Petersburg" — *Southern Living*, May 1967), but information on the disastrous movie for which the big boat was built had to come from John Douglas Eames's studio history *The MGM Story* (New York: Crown Publishers, 1985). The ill-fated Cape Coral Gardens park is practically a lost chapter in tourism history, but details on its fate were provided in an interview with Marbie Geller of the Cape Coral, Florida, Historical Museum. Inasmuch as most previous Florida histories chose to ignore the state's panhandle, a trip to the Bay County Library in Panama City was necessary. Their limited archives turned up two vintage anonymous articles of great historical significance: "The Gulf Beach" (*Panama City [Fla.] Pilot,* June 18, 1908) and "Six New Cottages to Be Built Near the 'Y'" (*Panama City Pilot,* October 22, 1936). A more recent historical account of the area's development was Marlene Womack's "Dream and 'Piece of Sand' Were Foundation for Panama City Beach," (*[Panama City] News Herald,* September 6, 1992). An undated clipping from the *News Herald,* "Couple Witness Growth of the Beach," by Phil Davis, gave a perspective on the strip's commercial development. A more negative view of the same development is Tom Fiedler's "Bay County: Much More than the Redneck Riviera" (*Beach-Bay News,* October 13, 1993). The history of Panama City Beach's futuristic (and now, past) tower was related in an interview with Val Valentine. My own childhood memories were the source of the giant Icee cups that lined the PCB strip, but Jim Johnstone of the Icee Corporation confirmed that they did exist at one time. The other resort communities of the Miracle Strip were given a history by Frank Craddock, an advertising executive in Pensacola, and the excellent compilation *Our Town,* edited by Tom Conner (Fort Walton Beach, Fla.: Northwest Florida Daily News, 1992). The fate of Destin's giant concrete Green Knight was described in an Associated Press story, "Destin's Roadside Sentinel Coming Down for New Mall," on April 27, 1993. Tourist literature and personal memories had to suffice for the non-Florida beaches of the South, although Jim Clark of Nashville, Tennessee, should be credited for the inclusion of Pirateland in Myrtle Beach, South Carolina.

Chapter 4

A most unusual source provided most of the data about early literature concerning the Southern mountains. This was Brian Walker's *Barney Google & Snuffy Smith: 75 Years of an American Legend* (Wilton, Conn.: Comicana Books, 1994), which deals with the subject in some detail.

Several excellent books describing the history of *The Grand Ole Opry* radio show are available, but one of the best is *Nashville's Grand Ole Opry: The First 50 Years* by Jack Hurst (New York: Abradale Press, 1975). Information on the mountains of Arkansas and their attractions came primarily from brochures and other such publications, but Donnie Pitchford of Carthage, Texas, crawled out of the woodwork with some further facts on Mountain Village 1890. Some excellent details on commercial development in the Ozarks can be found in Lisa Moore Larson's "Ozarks Harmony" (*National Geographic,* April 1998). Shirley Coleman of the Roanoke, Virginia, Chamber of Commerce lit up when asked the history of that city's famous electric star on Mill Mountain. Mary Jaeger-Gale of Chimney Rock Park keeps that attraction's historical fires burning, and some anonymous staff members at Grandfather Mountain provided the keys necessary to unlock the secrets of its past. The early history of the Great Smoky Mountains National Park and its environs can be found in Ed Trout's *Gatlinburg: Cinderella City* (Pigeon Forge, Tenn.: Griffin Graphics, 1984). Unfortunately, this book leaves off at just about the time the area's goofiest attractions were getting started, so further details had to come from Gatlinburg's Anna Porter Public Library and veteran commercial photographer Gene Aiken. Believe it or not, the most complete history of Gatlinburg's Ripley's Museum comes from a slim booklet, *Ripley's Believe It Or Not Museum,* by D. R. Copperthwaite (New York: Ripley International, 1971), but museum curator Richard Wine-burger had a few amazing facts of his own to contribute. Kay Powell of the Pigeon Forge Department of Tourism and the staff of the Cherokee, North Carolina, Visitors' Center were able to point me in the direction of research on those two tourist meccas, but once again memory and memorabilia had to be the final authority on such matters. The story of Lookout Mountain has been looked up a bit more thoroughly, particularly in John Wilson's comprehensive *Lookout: The Story of an Amazing Mountain* (Chattanooga: John Wilson, 1977). A couple of newspaper clippings, one vintage and one fairly recent, gave a picture of both ends of the mountain's history: "New Concrete Road up Lookout Mtn. Will be Formally Opened at Midnight" (*Chattanooga News,* April 14, 1927) and "Incline Railway Turns 100" (Associated Press story, November 17, 1995).

Chapter 5

The story of Rock City Gardens' charming Fairyland Caverns was partially provided by the attraction's own unparalleled archive, but valuable additional tales were related by the sculptor, Jessie Schmid, in a rare personal interview. The South's other fairylands were a bit harder to pin

down (much like real fairies, one supposes), but photographer Gene Aiken had some remarks about the Fairyland of Pigeon Forge, and Fred Thumberg of Tampa, Florida's Fun Forest Park came through with a classic 1960s brochure from the days when they were also known as Fairyland. North Carolina's Land of Oz park was well described by Caleb Pirtle III in "We're Off to See the Wizard" (*Southern Living,* June 1971), and in Jay Scarfone and William Stillman's *The Wizard of Oz Collector's Treasury* (West Chester, Pa.: Schiffer Publishing, 1992). Cindy Keller of the Emerald Mountain residential development sent an update on the abandoned Oz park's present-day condition. A wonderful gentleman at Sugar Mill Gardens in Daytona Beach, Martin Wittbold, was responsible for digging up that park's former incarnation known as Bongoland and providing the dinosaur statue photos seen here. Up in Virginia, JoAnn Leight of Dinosaur Land provided saurian stories from their past. The first book to adequately document miniature golf's Southern origins was *Miniature Golf* by John Margolies, Nina Garfinkel, and Maria Reidelbach (New York: Abbeville Press, 1987). More puttering around is evident in the articles "Wacky World," by Jim Auchmutey (*Atlanta Journal-Constitution,* July 21, 1991), and "Miniature Golf on the Miracle Strip," by Yours Truly (*SCA Journal,* Fall 1995). Randy Koplin, son of Goofy Golf founder Lee Koplin, set the record straight on his father's many imitators, and Goofy Golf employees Alta Love and Bob Fleske had their own unique perspectives on the little links. Pigeon Forge's prehistoric Magic World was mostly documented by personal experience, but founder Jim Sidwell Sr. and Earlie Teaster of the Pigeon Forge Department of Tourism did answer some questions about the park's early days. In contrast, Magic World's *last* days were recounted in Lara Turner's article "24-Year-Old Attraction Is Closing" (*The Mountain Press* [Gatlinburg, Tenn.], September 2, 1995). The origins of the Six Flags theme parks were unfurled by Judith A. Adams in *The American Amusement Park Industry: A History of Technology & Thrills* (Boston: Twayne Publishers, 1991), and *The Essential Guide to Six Flags Theme Parks* by Tim O'Brien (Birmingham: Oxmoor House, 1996), but the early days of the chain's installment in Atlanta were touted in "Angus Wynne Jr. Raises Six Flags Over Georgia" (*Southern Living,* June 1967), as well as my own visits there in my much younger years. To understand the late Dogpatch USA requires some familiarity with the comic strip upon which it was based, and a highly recommended collection of those strips is *Li'l Abner: Dailies, 1934–1935* by Al Capp (Princeton, Wis.: Kitchen Sink Press, 1988). An analysis of the strip can be found in Arthur Asa Berger's *Li'l Abner: A Study in American Satire* (Jackson: University Press of Mississippi, 1994). Glorious versions of Dogpatch's germination and construction appeared in the local newspaper stories "Li'l Abner Creator Al Capp Arrives at Dogpatch Today" (*Harrison [Ark.] Daily Times,* October 2, 1967) and "Capp to Open Dogpatch" (*The Baxter Bulletin*

[Mountain Home, Ark.], May 16, 1968). A melancholy view of the park's slow spiral downward is provided by Rodger Lyle Brown with "In Arkansas, a Dogpatch Way Past Its Prime" (*Atlanta Journal-Constitution*, July 11, 1993). Only recently have roadside scholars begun paying attention to the giant statues that line major tourist routes, but two historians, Len Davidson of Philadelphia and Jim Hiett of Nashville, were busy privately documenting these monstrosities more than two decades ago. Eventually there emerged "The American Roadside Giant: Myth, Meaning, & Cultural Identity" by Kevin J. Patrick, in the *SCA Journal* (Spring/Summer 1995). George Clinton Thompson's "Vulcan: Birmingham's Man of Iron" (*Alabama Heritage,* Spring 1991) forged a place in history for that towering metalworker.

Chapter 6

The Southern battlefields have been discussed so often that there is very little left to research on them, but Point Park's famous Jessie Schmid sculptures made headlines in "Lookout Dioramas Given to Area History Museum" (*Chattanooga News-Free Press*, August 10, 1990.) John D. Woolever's article "Stone Mountain Park: It Isn't What Was Planned, It's More" (*Barr's Postcard News*, February 5, 1996) remains one of the best descriptions of Georgia's giant granite glob from a tourism standpoint, although a much earlier account, "Watching Men Carve a Mountain" (*Southern Living*, February 1966), is also valuable because of its place in the park's timeline. A circle of sources were rounded up to become the history of Atlanta's Cyclorama painting, but Todd Smith of Rock City Gardens came up with most of the story on Chattanooga's Confederama (now known as the Battles for Chattanooga Museum). Uncle Remus author Joel Chandler Harris's days in Eatonton and Atlanta were detailed in Paul M. Cousins's thorough *Joel Chandler Harris: A Biography* (Baton Rouge: Louisiana State University Press, 1968), and were supplemented for this book by the staff of the Uncle Remus Museum. Tourist literature gave the abbreviated histories of Williamsburg, Virginia, and St. Augustine, Florida, and the attractions that operated therein. Dottie Locke of Potter's Wax Museum in St. Augustine was responsible for that venerable establishment's inclusion here. The phenomenon of the Southern outdoor drama had to be scripted from the plays' own promotional material, but an excellent overview was the article "Outdoor Dramas Recreate History" (*Southern Living*, July 1966). Had it not been for Richard Kelly's research done for *The Andy Griffith Show* (Winston-Salem, N.C.: John F. Blair, 1981), Andy's tenure as part of *The Lost Colony* might be as lost as the colony of the title. Much of the real-life drama behind the Battle of Horseshoe Bend came from *The Story of Alabama: A State History* by Joseph Parks and Robert Moore (Atlanta: Turner Smith & Co., 1952).

"Ships of State" (*Southern Living,* June 1968) gave berth to the section on drydocked vessels. The best epistle on Ave Maria Grotto sculptor Joseph Zoettl is a booklet entitled *Sermons In Stone: The Life and Work of Brother Joseph* (Chicago: Curt Teich & Co., 1965), A revised standard version appeared as "Ave Maria Grotto: The Little World of Brother Joe" (*Southern Living,* June 1966).

Chapter 7

Magnolia Gardens, Bellingrath Gardens, and Callaway Gardens all had their histories recorded in their promotional literature years ago, so there was very little left to learn about their blossoming reputations. When it comes to historic preservation, though, probably no tourist attraction in the world can compete with Rock City Gardens. Through the courtesy of Bill Chapin and Todd Smith, I was allowed access to enough Rock City history to fill a book of its own . . . but that's another story. One of Rock City's closest imitators also shared some of the lime(stone)light in "Horse Pens Gets Restored Just As It Was" by Rose Livingston (*The Birmingham News,* September 2, 1995). Cypress Gardens' press kit, sent by Robyn DeRidder of the publicity department, did most of the work of documenting their flowery past. "Virginia's Natural Bridge" (*Southern Living,* September 1966) joined forces with some early 1930s brochures to solidify that attraction's history. *Lookout: The Story of an Amazing Mountain* by John Wilson (Chattanooga: John Wilson, 1977), cited for chapter 4, brought together the elements that made up the story of Canyon Land Park. No greater story of the Okefenokee Swamp could be found than Dot Rees Gibson's *The Okefenokee: Land of the Trembling Earth* (Waycross, Ga.: Dot Gibson Publications, 1974), but the marsh's effect on cartoonist Walt Kelly (and vice versa) is best sketched in *Pogo Files for Pogophiles* by Selby Daley Kelly and Steve Thompson (Richfield, Minn.: Spring Hollow Books, 1992). Two articles gave the lowdown on cave attractions: "See the South Underground" (*Southern Living,* June 1966) and Carl H. Giles's "Sites Under the South Draw Millions" (*Southern Living,* May 1969). The discovery of Ruby Falls is covered in a little jewel of a volume, *The History of Ruby Falls* by Ed Brinkley (Chattanooga: E. B. Brinkley, 1964). Finally, two more features that put a new spin on spelunking are "Found: The Lost Sea" (*Southern Living,* November 1968) and "Plans Eyed for Cathedral Caverns" (Associated Press story, February 27, 1996.)

Chapter 8

More than any other, this chapter depended almost entirely on personal memory and material that would now fall under the classification of collectibles. The earliest version of Silver Springs' history appeared in *Shrine of the Water Gods* by Carita Doggett Corse (Silver Springs, Fla.: n.p., 1935). Historical data on both Silver Springs and Weeki Wachee Springs was provided by Steve Specht, who served as publicity director for both. Rainbow Springs State Park colored in some gaps in that attraction's past, but for the rest of the springs, history seems to have been given the deep six.

Chapter 9

It took quite a bit of hacking through the underbrush to get the story on the South's jungle attractions, but to the rescue came Janet Alford of McKee Jungle Gardens and Beverly Hunter of Sarasota Jungle Gardens. Judith A. Adams brewed up a brief account of Busch Gardens in her aforementioned book *The American Amusement Park Industry: A History of Technology & Thrills* (Boston: Twayne Publishers, 1991), but Busch's Michael Goldstein put some extra feathers in the nest. Jungle Larry's Safari would have been lost in quicksand had it not been for the help of JL's widow, Nancy Jane Tetzlaff. Vincent "Val" Valentine, the creative genius behind Panama City Beach's Jungle Land volcano, proved that he could give a complete account of that attraction's history without blowing a lot of smoke. The Western parks were almost as difficult to round up. It would seem that nothing at all has ever been published examining this subject, so for the story of these two-bit towns I had to go directly to their original pioneers: Chris Robbins (Tweetsie Railroad/Goldrush Junction), R. B. Coburn (Ghost Town/Six Gun Territory/Frontier Land), Randy Koplin (Tombstone Territory), and Paul Churchwell (Petticoat Junction). In addition, Ellen Long of Pigeon Forge's Dollywood theme park kept me abreast of the changes that attraction has undergone since its Rebel Railroad beginnings. You know what? I think I need a vacation!

Illustration Credits

Unless otherwise indicated, illustrations are from the author's personal collection.

Title page: Cartoon © 1961 by Charles F. Clark; used by permission. Page 2: Dana Abston Collection. Page 4: Postcard folder by H. & W. B. Drew Co. Page 5: Linen postcard folder by Eli Witt Co. Page 6: Linen postcard by Curt Teich Co., 1951. Page 10, top right: Chrome postcard by Curt Teich Co., 1960s. Page 10, bottom right: Chrome postcard by Bishop Printing & Litho Co., Marla Akin Collection. Page 11: Detail from Gulf Oil Co. map of Florida. Page 14, right: Chrome postcard by Robinsons Color Press. Page 17: Rock City Gardens Collection. Page 20: Chrome postcard by Dexter Press. Page 22: Linen postcard by Curt Teich Co., 1934, Marla Akin Collection. Page 23: Bay County Library Collection, Panama City, Fla. Page 24, left: Southern Living archives. Page 26: Chrome postcard by Dexter Press. Page 28, top and bottom right: Cora Saxon Collection. Page 29: Linen postcard by Colourpicture. Page 30: Chrome postcard by Dukane Press. Page 33, top left: Linen postcard by Advertising Products Co. Page 33, bottom right: Chrome postcard by Curt Teich Co., 1958. Page 34, top left: Detail from chrome postcard by Lin Caufield Co. Page 34, bottom right: Detail from chrome postcard by Dexter Press. Page 35, top and bottom left: Gene Aiken Collection. Page 36: Linen postcard by Curt Teich Co., 1941, Marla Akin Collection. Page 37: Chrome postcard by MWM Color Litho. Page 38, top right: Linen postcard by Bone-Crow Co. Page 38, bottom right: Linen postcard by Colourpicture. Page 39: Linen postcard by Curt Teich Co., 1938, Marla Akin Collection. Page 41: Photo by Oscar Plaster, National Lum & Abner Society Collection. Page 44, top left: Linen postcard by Tichnor Bros. Page 44, bottom right: Linen postcard by Tichnor Bros., Marla Akin Collection. Page 45, left: Brian Rucker Collection. Page 45, right: Detail from chrome postcard by Dexter Press. Page 46: Postcard folder, © 1955 Curt Teich Co. Page 49, top left: Postcard folder by Curt Teich Co. Page 49, bottom left: Linen postcard by Curt Teich Co., 1947. Page 50: Postcard folder, © 1942 Curt Teich Co. Page 52, right: Brian Rucker Collection. Page 55: Linen postcard by Tichnor Bros. Page 56, top right: Postcard folder, © 1955 Curt Teich Co. Page 56, bottom right: Linen postcard by Curt Teich Co., 1941. Page 59: Photo by Johnson, 1970, used by permission of Florida State Archives. Page 60: Jeri Good Collection. Page 61: Photo by Johnson, 1967, used by permission of Florida State Archives. Page 63, top left: Postcard folder by Tichnor Bros. Page 65: Linen postcard by Curt Teich Co., 1938. Page 66: Gene Aiken Collection. Page 69: Chrome postcard by Colourpicture. Page 70: Linen postcard by Curt Teich Co., 1920s, Rex Riffle Collection. Page 71: Linen postcard by Colourpicture, Rex Riffle Collection. Page 72: Linen postcard by Curt Teich Co., 1939. Page 73, bottom left: Linen postcard by Asheville Postcard Co. Page 74, bottom right: Linen postcard by Colourpicture. Page 76, bottom right: Linen postcard by Asheville Postcard Co. Page 77, top and bottom left: Linen postcards by E. C. Kropp Co. Page 83: Linen postcard by Tichnor Bros. Page 86: Postcard folder, © 1942 Curt Teich Co. Page 88: Linen postcard by Curt Teich Co., 1947. Page 90: Chrome postcard by Colourpicture. Page 91, bottom right: Photo by Hugh Morton, chrome postcard by Colourpicture. Page 92: Linen postcard by Curt Teich Co., 1950, Marla Akin Collection. Page 95, top and bottom left: Photos by Martin Wittbold. Page 95, bottom right: Chrome postcard by Colourpicture, courtesy of Dinosaur Land. Page 97, bottom right: Photo by W. M. Cline Co. Page 98: Southern Living archives. Page 99, bottom right: Chrome postcard by Dexter Press, © 1967 Great Southwest Corp. Used by permission of Six Flags Over Georgia. Page 101: Postcard folder by Dexter Press. Page 102: Chrome postcard by Dexter Press. Page 106: Linen postcards by Curt Teich Co., 1936 and 1938. Page 109, left: Postcard folder and linen postcard by R & R News Co. Page 111: Brochure © 1966 by City of Atlanta. Page 112: Ed Tennyson Collection. Page 113, left: Chrome postcard by W. M. Cline Co. Page 114: Postcard folder, © 1939 Curt Teich Co. Page 115, bottom right: Linen postcard by Curt Teich Co., 1939. Page 117, left: Ed Tennyson Collection. Page 121, right: Chrome postcard by W. M. Cline Co. Page 122: Chrome postcard by W. M. Cline Co. Page 123: Chrome postcard by Alabama Postcard Co. Page 126: Postcard folder, © 1941 Curt Teich Co. Page 128, left: Linen postcard by K. S. Tanner Co. Page 129, bottom right: Linen postcard by Curt Teich Co., 1935. Page 132, left: Chrome postcard by Alabama Postcard Co., Steve Gilmer Collection. Page 132, right: Postcard folder by Asheville Postcard Co. Page 133: Used by permission of Cypress Gardens. Page 134: Linen postcard by Curt Teich Co., 1952. Page 135: Postcard folder, © 1962 Curt Teich Co. Page 136: Chrome postcard by Curt Teich Co., 1962. Page 141: Photo by W. M. Cline Co. Page 144: Linen postcard by Curt Teich Co., 1947. Page 146: Photo © 1994 Silver Springs, used by permission. Page 148, left: Val Valentine Collection. Page 148, right: Linen postcard by Curt Teich Co., 1941. Page 149, left and right: Linen postcards by Curt Teich Co., 1938 and 1949. Page 151: Photo by Ted Lagerberg. Page 152: Photo by Ted Lagerberg, chrome postcard by Florida Natural Color. Page 153, left and right: Chrome postcards by Florida Natural Color. Page 154: Linen postcard by Curt Teich Co., 1948. Page 156: Linen postcard by Curt Teich Co., McKee Botanical Gardens Collection. Page 158, top right: Linen postcard by Curt Teich Co. Page 158, bottom right: Chrome postcard by Dexter Press. Page 161, left: Used by permission of Florida State Archives. Page 161, right: Val Valentine Collection. Page 163: Chrome postcard by Dexter Press. Page 165: Ed Tennyson Collection. Page 167, left: Chrome postcard by Colourpicture. Page 167, right: Photo by Dodson, Craddock, & Borne Advertising. Page 168, bottom right: Courtesy of Bay County Library, Panama City, Fla.

Index